Macarena Hernández Salmerón
Diego Romero-Ávila

Convergence in Output and Its Sources Among Industrialised Countries

A Cross-Country Time-Series Perspective

Springer

Macarena Hernández Salmerón
Economics, Innovation, Science and Employment Department
Regional Government of Andalusia
Sevilla
Spain

Diego Romero-Ávila
Department of Economics, Quantitative Methods and Economic History
Pablo de Olavide University
Sevilla
Spain

ISSN 2191-5504 ISSN 2191-5512 (electronic)
SpringerBriefs in Economics
ISBN 978-3-319-13634-9 ISBN 978-3-319-13635-6 (eBook)
DOI 10.1007/978-3-319-13635-6

Library of Congress Control Number: 2014956711

JEL classification: C23, O5

Springer Cham Heidelberg New York Dordrecht London

Printed on acid-free paper

Springer International Publishing AG Switzerland is part of Springer Science+Business Media (www.springer.com)

SpringerBriefs in Economics

More information about this series at http://www.springer.com/series/8876

Acknowledgments

The authors would like to thank Jesús Crespo-Cuaresma, Miguel León-Ledesma, Daniel Oto-Peralías, Carlos Usabiaga and Simon Wren-Lewis for valuable comments and suggestions. Diego Romero-Ávila acknowledges financial support from the Spanish Ministry of Science and Technology through grant ECO2009-13357, the Spanish Ministry of Economics and Competitiveness through grant ECO2012-35430 and the Andalusian Council of Innovation and Science under Excellence Project SEJ-4546.

Contents

Abstract

This study investigates the existence of stochastic and deterministic convergence of real output per worker and the sources of output (physical capital per worker, human capital per worker, total factor productivity—TFP—and average annual hours worked) in 21 OECD countries over the period 1970–2011. Towards this end, we apply a large battery of panel unit root and stationarity tests, all robust to the presence of cross-sectional dependence. The evidence fails to provide clear-cut evidence of convergence dynamics either in real GDP per worker or in the series of the sources of output. Except for the panel unit root tests of Choi (2002) and Moon and Perron (2004), the panel unit root statistics of Chang (2002), Smith et al. (2004), Breitung and Das (2005) and Pesaran (2007) as well as the panel stationarity tests of Hadri (2000) and Harris et al. (2005) do not generally support the convergence hypothesis. Due to some limitations associated with the above panel unit root and stationarity tests, we use the more flexible PANIC approach of Bai and Ng (2004a) which provides evidence that real GDP per worker, real physical capital per worker, human capital and average annual hours exhibit some degree of deterministic convergence, whereas TFP series display a high degree of stochastic convergence.

Keywords Time-series convergence · Cross-sectional dependence · Bootstrap distribution · Factor models · PANIC

Chapter 1
Introduction

Abstract This chapter describes the different notions of cross-section and time-series convergence as well as presents a brief literature review of the main studies in the field of convergence and a brief account of their results. It also motivates the present study that investigates the existence of stochastic and deterministic convergence of real output per worker and its sources in 21 OECD countries over the period 1970–2011. It argues that the application of a large battery of panel unit root and stationarity tests, all robust to the presence of cross-sectional dependence, enables us to be more confident that non-rejections of the null of a unit root are not caused by the low power of conventional unit root tests of the ADF-type. A major novelty of our study compared to previous ones is that we investigate the existence of convergence patterns in the series of physical capital per worker, human capital, total factor productivity and average annual hours worked, which constitute the main sources of output.

Keywords Time-series convergence · Literature review · Introduction

The increasing availability of cross-country datasets, such as the Penn World Table developed by Summers and Heston (1991) and the long-term real per capita GDP data by Maddison (2003), has enabled researchers to investigate empirically cross-country income convergence as well as to make international comparisons of living standards over extended periods of time. In addition, the different predictions of neoclassical growth theory pioneered by the work of Solow (1956) and the endogenous growth models of Romer (1986, 1990) and Lucas (1988), among others, regarding cross-country convergence dynamics have given rise to an intense debate among economists, economic historians and policy makers on the existence of income convergence across countries and regions. Under neoclassical growth theory, diminishing returns to reproducible capital lead inevitably to convergence due to the flow of capital to those economies with relatively lower capital to labour ratios. In contrast, under endogenous growth theory, the presence of constant or increasing returns to reproducible capital supports the existence of cross-country income divergence.

M. Hernández Salmerón and D. Romero-Ávila, *Convergence in Output and Its Sources Among Industrialised Countries*,
SpringerBriefs in Economics, DOI 10.1007/978-3-319-13635-6_1

Several indicators of cross-sectional convergence are emphasised in the literature. β-convergence implies that countries starting from a high level of output are expected to exhibit lower output growth than countries beginning with low output levels.[1] In addition, σ-convergence tracks the inter-temporal change in a measure of dispersion such as the standard deviation or the coefficient of variation. This definition aims at establishing whether there is a tendency for cross-country income differences to decline over time. However, cross-section tests of β-convergence are problematic since they (1) tend to over-reject the null of no convergence when countries are characterised by different steady states (Bernard and Durlauf 1996); (2) may render evidence of conditional convergence even when cross-country income distributions remain unaltered over time (Quah 1993); and (3) require to have identical first-order autoregressive dynamic structures across countries as well as to control for all factors causing cross-country steady-state income differentials (Evans and Karras 1996).

These shortcomings can be overcome, at least in part, by employing time series methods. This is the purpose of the approach taken by Carlino and Mills (1993) who proposed the notion of stochastic convergence. This notion of convergence implies that shocks to per capita income levels relative to the average of the group are temporary, thus leading the series to revert towards their respective equilibrium level of relative income. As pointed out by Li and Papell (1999), the notion of stochastic convergence implies that the log of relative income is trend stationary, and thus constitutes a weak notion of convergence. This is due to the fact that it allows for time-varying permanent differences in per capita income levels across countries through the presence of a linear trend in the deterministic component of the trend function. As a result, Li and Papell (1999) proposed a stronger definition of convergence, called deterministic convergence, which implies that the log of relative income is mean stationary. Therefore, the elimination of both the deterministic and stochastic trends entails that income levels in one country move in parallel over the long run relative to average levels. Thus, deterministic convergence implies stochastic convergence, but not the other way around. According to Oxley and Greasley (1995), these two degrees of convergence can be conceived as: (1) catching-up in the case of stochastic convergence, which views convergence as an ongoing process of narrowing of the income gap among economies that have not yet converged; (2) long-run convergence in the case of deterministic convergence, which refers to the case in which countries attain full convergence to their respective steady-state equilibrium incomes. Besides, Bernard and Durlauf (1995) propose an even stronger notion of convergence which requires stationarity with zero mean in the relative output series.

These different approaches have tended to provide contradictory results regarding the convergence hypothesis. On the one hand, cross-section tests provide evidence of

[1] The terms conditional and unconditional (absolute) refer to whether convergence takes place after controlling or not for country-specific characteristics, which explain cross-country differences in steady state income levels.

absolute β-convergence for U.S. regions, Western European regions and Japanese prefectures (Barro and Sala-i-Martin 1992, 1995), and for OECD economies (Baumol 1986; Dowrick and Nguyen 1989; De Long 1988; Islam 1995). Likewise, cross-section tests support the conditional β-convergence hypothesis for the OECD as well as for large samples of countries (Mankiw et al. 1992; Barro 1991). Regarding the testing of time series notions of convergence, we find three main groups of studies on the basis of the type of unit root and stationarity tests used to investigate the convergence hypothesis. First, early time series tests employing univariate unit root techniques, generally of the augmented Dickey-Fuller (1979)—ADF hereafter—type generally failed to reject the null of no convergence for U.S. regions (Carlino and Mills 1993), for OECD countries (Bernard and Durlauf 1995), and for large international samples (Quah 1992; Ben-David 1994). It is thus not surprising that these results from univariate unit root tests have gone challenged. Christiano and Eichenbaum (1990), De Jong et al. (1992) and Rudebusch (1993) stress that standard univariate unit root tests have low power in distinguishing between a trend stationary and a unit root process, particularly for short spans of data.

This has resulted in two separate strategies as a means to raise statistical power when testing time series notions of convergence. Thus, in a second group of studies, researchers have followed the seminal work of Perron (1989) and controlled for structural change in the deterministic component of the trend function of relative income levels. This ensures that results are not biased towards the non-rejection of the null of no convergence due to misinterpretation of stationarity with a structural break as a unit root. As a matter of fact, Loewy and Papell (1996) incorporate an endogenously determined structural break in sequential trend break models and provide some evidence of stochastic convergence in seven of the eight U.S. regions, as opposed to only three regions exhibiting convergence in Carlino and Mills' analysis. These results are corroborated by Tomljanovich and Vogelsang (2002) who tested for time-series β-convergence in the U.S. regions through robust trend tests allowing for an endogenous structural break in the specification. Employing similar testing methods to Loewy and Papell (1996), Li and Papell (1999) find the existence of deterministic convergence for 10, and stochastic convergence for 14, of the 16 OECD countries analysed over the period 1900–1989. Using a two-break Lagrange Multiplier (LM) unit root test to study stochastic convergence in 15 OECD countries over the period 1870–1994, Strazicich et al. (2004) find support for convergence in most countries. Along similar lines, employing a one-break unit root test for per capita GDP over the period 1900–2001, Dawson and Sen (2007) provide evidence of stochastic convergence in 21 of the 29 countries analysed. All these studies find that most structural breaks detected coincide with World War II, which may be the cause of a major break in the convergence process.[2]

[2] Employing multivariate time-series techniques, Attfield (2003) investigates convergence in seven European countries from 1980. He finds evidence of stochastic convergence in five countries after allowing for a structural break in the cointegrating space.

In a third group of studies, researchers have turned to a panel approach, which raises statistical power by exploiting the cross-sectional variability of the data. This constitutes a more efficient way to achieve important power gains. Using the panel unit root test of Levin et al. (2002), Evans and Karras (1996) provide evidence consistent with stochastic convergence for the states of the U.S. over the period 1929–1991, as well as for 54 countries over the period 1950–1990. Cheung and Pascual (2004) employ several panel unit root and stationarity tests without breaks and provide mixed evidence of stochastic convergence among the Group of Seven countries over the postwar era, while some favourable evidence of convergence over the 20th century. Using three panel unit root tests without breaks, Fleissig and Strauss (2001) are unable to provide evidence of stochastic convergence for 15 OECD economies and a European sub-sample over the period 1900–1987, whereas the results favour convergence for the period 1948–1987. Hence, they argue for the existence of large infrequent shifts in the relative output series, which may be responsible for the failure to reject the no convergence null hypothesis for the entire period. More recently, using the panel stationarity test that allows for multiple breaks developed by Carrion-i-Silvestre et al. (2005), Romero-Ávila (2009) investigates the existence of convergence for a sample of 19 OECD countries over the period 1870–2003. The evidence favours convergence in output over the 20th century.

This paper investigates the existence of stochastic and deterministic convergence of real output per worker and the sources of output (real physical capital per worker, human capital per worker, total factor productivity—TFP—and average annual hours worked) in 21 countries over the period 1970–2011. Towards this end, we apply a large battery of panel unit root and stationarity tests, all robust to the presence of cross-sectional dependence. By using these panel tests we can be more confident that non-rejections of the null of a unit root are not caused by the low power of conventional unit root tests such as the ADF or Phillips-Perron (1988) tests. A major novelty of our study compared to previous ones is that we investigate the existence of convergence patterns in the series of physical capital per worker, human capital, TFP and average annual hours worked, which constitute the main sources of output.[3] As noted by Miller and Upadhyay (2002), the analysis of convergence of TFP can give an idea of the cross-boundary adoption and

[3] There are two exceptions to this. Miller and Upadhyay (2002) test for β-absolute convergence of real GDP per worker and TFP for a sample of 83 countries over the period 1960–1989 through cross-section regressions as well as for conditional convergence via fixed-effects estimation. Their findings support both absolute and conditional convergence of TFP, but only conditional convergence of labor productivity. Grier and Grier (2007) investigate the existence of σ-convergence in output per worker and investment rates of physical and human capital for a sample of 90 countries over 1961–1999 as well as for a subsample of 22 rich countries. Whereas both output per capita and investment rates appear to converge in the sample of rich countries, in the full sample investment rates converge but per capita output diverges.

convergence of technological advances (see also Bernard and Jones 1996a). They also point out that the finding of convergence in TFP indicates that technology is a public good that can quickly cross international boundaries.

It is worth noting that testing for cross-sectional dependence in the data is important because (1) when cross-sectional correlation is not present in the data, panel unit root tests allowing for it may suffer from a substantial loss of power, and (2) standard panel tests that fail to allow for cross-sectional dependence, when present, exhibit dramatic size distortions (see O'Connell 1998; Maddala and Wu 1999; Strauss and Yigit 2003; Banerjee et al. 2005). Therefore, unlike most previous studies and given the importance of correctly identifying the presence of cross-dependence, we conduct a formal analysis of the prevalence of cross-dependence in our panels of real GDP per worker, real physical capital per worker, human capital, TFP and average annual hours worked by employing the CD test of error cross-dependence recently developed by Pesaran (2004).

Since the CD test indicates the existence of cross-sectional dependencies in the innovations forming the panels studied, we employ in our analysis the recently developed panel unit root tests of Choi (2002), Chang (2002), Smith et al. (2004), Moon and Perron (2004), Breitung and Das (2005) and Pesaran (2007), which explicitly allow for cross-sectional dependence. Smith et al. (2004) control for general forms of cross-sectional dependence through modified bootstrap methods, rendering tests with good size and power. Breitung and Das (2005) control for weak cross-sectional dependence through seemingly-unrelated methods, and Chang (2002) allows for cross-correlation by using a nonlinear instrumental variables (IV) method. The other panel procedures assume a common factor structure to explain the evolution of the observed series. Whereas the panel unit root test by Choi (2002) considers a restrictive one-factor model in which all cross-sectional units are equally affected by the common factor, and Pesaran's (2007) tests also allow for one common factor but with different factor loadings across units, the panel statistics of Moon and Perron (2004) are more general because they allow for more than one common factor.

Since most of the existing panel unit root tests—including the ones employed in our analysis—are constructed in a way that rejection of the null hypothesis of joint nonstationarity tells us only that some but not all cross-sectional units are stationary,[4] it is advisable to complement that analysis with panel tests that take joint stationarity as the null hypothesis. This is because, as forcefully argued by Shin and Snell (2006), the use of panel unit root tests in combination with panel stationarity tests may lead to definitive conclusions about the stochastic properties of the variable under study. First, when there is rejection of the null with the panel stationarity test but not with the panel unit root test, it implies that all cross-sectional units contain a unit root. Second, when there is rejection with the panel unit root test

[4] In our case, all the panel unit root tests, with the exception of those of Moon and Perron (2004), take the null hypothesis of a unit root in all panel members versus the alternative of stationarity in at least one cross-sectional unit. In contrast, Moon and Perron's statistics take stationarity in all panel members as the alternative hypothesis.

but not with the panel stationarity test, there is stationarity in all cross-sectional units.[5] Also related, Taylor and Sarno (1998) and Karlsson and Lothgren (2000), demonstrate through Monte Carlo simulations that heterogeneous panel unit root tests are likely to reject the joint nonstationarity null even when there is a single stationary but persistent series in a system otherwise nonstationary. Under these circumstances, it makes more sense to have stationarity as the null hypothesis to be tested, since failure to reject the null in this case would imply that all countries are stochastically converging.[6] The analysis with panel stationarity tests can also act as confirmatory of previous work that investigates time series notions of convergence in OECD countries through univariate as well as panel tests taking non-stationarity as the null hypothesis such as Li and Papell (1999), Fleissig and Strauss (2001), Strazicich et al. (2004) and Dawson and Sen (2007).

Therefore, to conduct such a confirmatory analysis we complement the use of panel unit root tests with the panel stationarity tests proposed by Hadri (2000) and Harris et al. (2005). The former is computed as an average of individual Kwiatkowski et al. (1992, KPSS) tests. Since the asymptotic distribution of Hadri's test assumes cross-sectional independence, we allow for general forms of cross-sectional dependence by simulating the bootstrap distribution of the test following Maddala and Wu (1999). The panel stationarity test by Harris et al. (2005) is general enough to allow for several common factors as a way to control for strong forms of cross-sectional dependence.

Note that, for the sake of simplicity, we employ panel unit root and stationarity tests that do not explicitly allow for breaks because the analysis covers the period 1970–2011. Thus, by excluding major events such as the two World Wars and the Great Depression, the need to control for structural breaks diminishes. In addition, if we were to allow for breaks in the analysis, the trimming of the initial portion of the time span would not allow us to identify any breaks associated with the oil shocks of the 1970s. For this reason, we prefer to focus on panel procedures that do not control for structural breaks. Moreover, the large majority of the panel unit root and stationarity tests employed in the empirical analysis, though robust to cross-correlation, have not been extended to the case of unknown breaks in the trend function.

Overall, the analysis fails to provide clear-cut evidence of convergence (either stochastic or deterministic) either in real GDP per worker or in the series constituting the sources of output. Except for the panel unit root tests of Choi (2002) and Moon and Perron (2004), the other panel unit root statistics of Chang (2002), Smith et al. (2004), Breitung and Das (2005) and Pesaran (2007) as well as the panel stationarity tests of Hadri (2000) and Harris et al. (2005) do not generally support the convergence hypothesis.

---

[5] The other two cases are when there is rejection in both panel unit root and stationarity tests, which would indicate the existence of a mixture of stationarity and nonstationarity in the panel, whereas failure to reject the null in both tests could lead to inconclusive inferences.

[6] Kuo and Mikkola (2001) and Bai and Ng (2004b) apply similar arguments to the analysis of the Purchasing Power Parity question.

In order to overcome some limitations associated with the above panel unit root and stationarity tests, we then apply the less restrictive framework given by Panel Analysis of Non-stationarity in Idiosyncratic and Common components (PANIC) recently developed by Bai and Ng (2004a). The application of these techniques enables us to provide more clear-cut evidence regarding the empirical validity of the two notions of convergence in the OECD. Overall, the analysis of stochastic convergence provides strong evidence of convergence patterns in the series of log TFP, as given by the existence of pairwise convergence among individual series, as well as weaker evidence of convergence in real GDP per worker and average annual hours worked (which exhibited two common stochastic trends) and yet weaker evidence of convergence in real physical capital per worker and human capital (which exhibited three common stochastic trends). As for the analysis of deterministic convergence, there is some evidence of convergence in real GDP per worker and average annual hours worked, and to a lower extent in real physical capital per worker and human capital, but the evidence for log TFP points to a lack of deterministic convergence.

The rest of the study is structured as follows. Chapter 2 describes the empirical strategy and the data used. Chapter 3 presents the econometric methods employed in the analysis. Chapter 4 reports the results of the analysis of stochastic and deterministic convergence in real GDP per worker, real physical capital per worker, human capital, TFP and average annual hours worked across OECD economies. Chapter 5 presents the main limitations associated with the application of the panel unit root and stationarity tests used in Chap. 4 for the analysis of time-series convergence. It also describes an alternative and less restrictive framework based on PANIC methods. Chapter 6 reports the results obtained from the application of the PANIC approach to the log of the series. Chapter 7 concludes the study.

Chapter 2
Model Specification and Data

Abstract This chapter outlines the empirical framework and the main variables involved in the analysis of stochastic and deterministic convergence. It then describes the data source used and the exact data series employed to measure real output per worker, real physical capital per worker, human capital, total factor productivity (TFP) and average annual hours worked. As regards the data source, we employ the newest version of the so-called Penn World Table, version 8.0. As measures of real GDP, real physical capital and TFP, we employ the series based on national-accounts data. As for the measure of human capital, we employ the Psacharopoulos (1994) survey of wage equations evaluating the returns to education that transforms average years of schooling data into a human capital index.

Keywords Real GDP per worker · Real physical capital per worker · Human capital · Total factor productivity · Annual hours worked · Penn world table 8.0

After introducing the topic and briefly reviewing the literature on output convergence, we now describe the empirical strategy and data employed in the analysis.

2.1 Model Specification and Definitions of Convergence

The starting point is a standard Cobb-Douglas production function with constant returns to scale on the inputs employed in production, as follows:

$$Y_{it} = A_{it} K_{it}^{\alpha} (h_{it} L_{it})^{1-\alpha} \tag{2.1}$$

where aggregate output Y_{it} is a function of A_{it} which accounts for TFP, the stock of physical capital K_{it}, and human capital augmented labor, which is the product of a human capital index h_{it} (accounting for the amount of human capital per worker) times raw labor given by L_{it}. α is the output elasticity of physical capital, and $1 - \alpha$

M. Hernández Salmerón and D. Romero-Ávila, *Convergence in Output and Its Sources Among Industrialised Countries*, SpringerBriefs in Economics, DOI 10.1007/978-3-319-13635-6_2

is the output elasticity of augmented labor.[1] The production function can be rewritten by expressing aggregate output and physical capital in per worker terms. This renders the following:

$$y_{it} = A_{it} k_{it}^{\alpha} h_{it}^{1-\alpha} \tag{2.2}$$

where y_{it} and k_{it} are output per worker and physical capital per worker, respectively. Applying natural logs to both sides of Eq. 2.2, it renders:

$$\ln y_{it} = \ln A_{it} + \alpha \ln k_{it} + (1-\alpha) \ln h_{it} \tag{2.3}$$

Equation 2.3 contains the main variables involved in the analysis of convergence conducted below. The aim is to investigate the existence of stochastic and deterministic convergence in output, but also to assess the convergence hypothesis in the main sources of output per worker, i.e. TFP, physical capital per worker, and human capital. This constitutes an important improvement over most of the literature on convergence that has focused only on the study of output convergence and hence neglected the analysis of convergence dynamics in the main sources of output.

Following common practice in the time-series convergence literature, we compute the logarithm of the ratio of country-specific per worker real GDP to the average per worker GDP for the sample of 21 OECD countries. Thus, the variable of interest for unit root testing is relative output levels, i.e. $RI_{it} = \ln\left(y_{it}/\bar{y}_t\right)$, where y_{it} represents individual country's real GDP per worker and $\bar{y}_t = \left(\sum_{i=1}^{N} y_{it}/N\right)$ stands for the average real GDP per worker of the group. $i = 1, \ldots, N$ stands for the number of countries and $t = 1, \ldots, T$ for the time periods. In our case, N equals 21 and T equals 42, thus making a balanced panel composed of 882 observations.

The same normalisation is applied to the stock of physical capital per worker, the human capital index, TFP and average annual hours worked per worker.[2] Hence, relative physical capital per worker is given by $RK_{it} = \ln(k_{it}/\bar{k}_t)$, where k_{it} represents individual country's real physical capital per worker and $\bar{k}_t = \left(\sum_{i=1}^{N} k_{it}/N\right)$ represents the average real physical capital per worker of the group. For relative human capital, we have $Rh_{it} = \ln(h_{it}/\bar{h}_t)$, with h_{it} representing individual country's human capital per worker and $\bar{h}_t = \left(\sum_{i=1}^{N} h_{it}/N\right)$ the average human capital of the group. As regards relative TFP, $RA_{it} = \ln(A_{it}/\bar{A}_t)$, with A_{it} standing for individual country's TFP and $\bar{A}_t = \left(\sum_{i=1}^{N} A_{it}/N\right)$ being the average TFP of the group. Regarding relative annual hours worked per worker engaged in production, $RH_{it} = \ln(H_{it}/\bar{H}_t)$, where

[1] As shown below, for the computation of the TFP series, Inklaar and Timmer (2013) approximate these output elasticities by assuming perfect competition in factor and good markets. This allows to consider α as the share of GDP not earned by labor.

[2] We include average annual hours worked in our convergence analysis because the production function could be written in terms of per hour worked rather than in per worker terms.

H_{it} stands for country-specific annual hours per worker and $\bar{H}_t = \left(\sum_{i=1}^{N} H_{it}/N\right)$ is the average annual hours per worker of the group.

By normalising country-specific series of real output per worker or its sources against the average of the respective series, we are able to distinguish country-specific movements from common trends in the respective variable caused by global shocks such as the oil crises of the seventies. However, since this procedure only allows for a very restrictive form of cross-correlation, we employ several methods to allow for general forms of cross-sectional dependence. This comprises the simulation of the bootstrap distribution tailored to the error structure of our panel of each respective series, the use of nonlinear IV or the utilisation of factor models, with the latter allowing for stronger forms of cross-correlation. In a nutshell, a unit root in the log of relative real GDP per worker implies divergence of the series from the average output per worker of the group. By way of contrast, stationarity in the log of relative real GDP per worker levels entails that shocks to real GDP per worker relative to the average affect the series only temporarily, which leads the series to converge after the effect of the shock vanishes. The same reason applies to the relative series constructed for real physical capital per worker, human capital per worker, TFP and average annual hours worked.

As noted by Li and Papell (1999), the concept of stochastic convergence, which implies that the log of relative output per worker is trend stationary, is a weak notion of convergence. This is due to the fact that it allows for permanent differences in per worker output levels across countries through the presence of a linear trend in the deterministic component of the trend function. As a response to that, Li and Papell (1999) propose a stronger definition of convergence, called deterministic convergence, which implies that the log of relative output per worker is mean stationary. For this to hold, it is necessary to eliminate both deterministic and stochastic trends, which would imply that output per worker in one country moves in parallel over the long run relative to average output per worker levels. One can thus infer that deterministic convergence implies stochastic convergence, but not the other way around.

For the sake of completeness, we study both time series definitions of convergence. However, we do not deal in detail with other definitions of convergence using cross-section data. The reasons for this are the following. Firstly, cross-sectional forms of convergence such as conditional β-convergence constitute a much weaker notion of convergence than time series convergence.[3] This stems from the fact that cross-section tests are subject to spurious rejections of the null of no convergence

---

[3] β-convergence implies that countries starting from a high income level are expected to exhibit lower income growth than countries beginning with low income levels. The terms conditional and unconditional (absolute) refer to whether convergence takes place after controlling or not for country-specific characteristics, which can account for differences in steady state income levels.

when economies exhibit differing steady states.[4] Secondly, Ericsson et al. (2001) show that the aggregation of data over several decades may hide convergence. The reverse could also be true, since aggregation may lead to spurious convergence. In addition, cross-section analysis confounds short-run dynamics with long-run features of the data. Thirdly, by taking a panel data approach, we exploit the time series and cross-section dimensions of the data. This allows us to control for conditional convergence through the inclusion of country-specific effects, which proxy for time-invariant compensating differentials among economies. Last but not least, by exploiting the panel dimension of the data, we can combine the transition and steady-state information contained in the cross-section and time-series approaches (Bernard and Durlauf 1996).

2.2 Data Description

Once we have outlined the empirical framework and the main variables involved in our analysis of stochastic and deterministic convergence, we now describe the data source used and the exact data series employed to measure output per worker, physical capital per worker, human capital, TFP and average annual hours worked. As regards the data source, we employ the newest version of the so-called Penn World Table, version 8.0 (henceforth PWT8.0), developed by the joint efforts of Robert Feenstra from the University of California at Davis, and Robert Inklaar and Marcel Timmer from the Groningen Growth and Development Centre at the University of Groningen (see Feenstra et al. 2013a, b, c).[5]

As a measure of aggregate output, we employ a measure of constant-price real GDP, denoted by $RGDP^{NA}$, which represents real GDP at constant 2005 national prices (in million 2005 US$). This series employs national-accounts growth rates to construct the real GDP series. This series is similar to those of the previous versions of the PWT, though some differences in its computation are pointed out by Feenstra et al. (2013a, b, c). In fact, versions of the PWT prior to 6.0 constructed the real GDP series using a weighted average of the national-accounts growth rates of the GDP components given by private consumption, investment and government consumption. This caused the real GDP growth rate in PWT to differ from the growth rate of real GDP in the national accounts due to these weights. This phenomenon was highly criticised by Jonhson et al. (2013) due to the fact that these weights differed across the different versions of PWT. This caveat was addressed by the authors in succeeding versions of PWT by using the national-accounts growth rate of total

[4] Bernard and Durlauf (1996) further demonstrate that a negative cross-section relationship between initial income and growth is compatible with a class of structural models which violate the time series definition of convergence implied by the equality of long-term forecasts of per capita output for two countries at a fixed time. Along similar lines, Quah (1993) shows that the existence of β-convergence is compatible with a stable cross-section variance in output levels.

[5] The data are accessible from www.ggdc.net/pwt.

GDP rather than that of the C, I and G components. This aggregate output series is comparable across countries and over time.

As regards the stock of physical capital, we employ the real stock of physical capital, denoted by RK^{NA} provided in PWT8.0. As Inklaar and Timmer (2013) point out, there are several clear advantages of using these series versus other physical capital stock series previously developed in the literature. First, this stock of physical capital series accounts for differences in asset composition across countries and over time. Hence, investment is split up into the following categories: structures, transport equipment and machinery, which in turn can be divided into investment in computers, communication equipment, software and other machinery. Thus, this improves over most previous physical capital estimates that assumed total investment in a single homogeneous asset for all countries. Second, an implication from the above is that the depreciation rate of physical capital exhibits variation across countries and over time —instead of assuming a constant depreciation rate—and that the PPP associated with the stocks of physical capital need not be equal to the investment PPP considered in the conventional approach. Third, in computing the initial stock of physical capital, Inklaar and Timmer (2013) replace the restrictive steady-state assumption by considering an initial capital/output ratio. As shown in specification (2.3), we need a measure of total employment to compute both real GDP and real physical capital in per worker terms. For that purpose, we use the employment series in PWT8.0, which tries to measure "the total number of persons engaged in a productive activity within the boundaries of the system of National Accounts. This should include all employees, but also self-employed workers, unpaid family workers that are economically engaged, apprentices and the military" (Inklaar and Timmer 2013, p. 35). Real physical capital per worker represents the stock of physical capital per worker at constant 2005 national prices (in million 2005 US$).

As far as the measure of human capital is concerned, we employ the human capital index in PWT8.0 obtained on the basis of average years of schooling data for the population aged 15 and over stemming from Barro and Lee (2010), version 1.3 covering the period 1950–2010. They adopt the Psacharopoulos (1994) survey of wage equations evaluating the returns to education to transform these average years of schooling data into a human capital index. In particular, let s_{it} represent the average number of years of education of the adult population in country i at time t and the human capital index be a function of the average number of years of education of the adult population as follows:

$$h_{it} = e^{\phi(s_{it})} \tag{2.4}$$

where h_{it} constitutes an index of human capital per worker. ϕ is a piecewise linear function, with a zero intercept and a slope of 0.134 through the 4th year of education, 0.101 for the next 4 years, and 0.068 for education beyond the 8th year.[6] Clearly, the rate of return to education (where ϕ is differentiable) is

---

[6] See Badunenko and Romero-Ávila (2013, 2014) for other studies employing a similar definition of human capital.

$$\frac{d \ln h_{it}}{ds_{it}} = \phi'(s_{it}) \tag{2.5}$$

As with the other series, the human capital index exhibits cross-country and time-series variability.

As regards the TFP series, we employ the index number provided in PWT8.0, denoted as $RTFP^{NA}$, which is associated with national accounts data and represents TFP at constant national prices (2005 = 1). This series is calculated as follows:

$$RTFP^{NA}_{t,t-1} = \frac{RGDP^{NA}_{t}}{RGDP^{NA}_{t-1}} \Big/ Q^{T}_{t,t-1} \tag{2.6}$$

where $RGDP^{NA}$ is national-accounts based real GDP per worker in PWT8.0 and Q^T is the Törnqvist quantity index of factor inputs (in this case physical capital per worker and human capital).

Since the production function could be expressed in terms of per hour worked instead of in per worker terms, we take advantage of the series of average annual hours worked per worker available in PWT8.0 and also assess whether there has been convergence or not in this measure of raw labour. This measure accounts for the average annual hours worked by persons engaged in productive activity.

In all, we use annual data on the variables described above for 21 OECD countries over the period 1970–2011, for which complete data series were available.[7] The countries under analysis are Australia, Austria, Belgium, Canada, Denmark, Finland, France, Germany, Greece, Ireland, Italy, Japan, the Netherlands, New Zealand, Norway, Portugal, Spain, Sweden, Switzerland, the United Kingdom and the United States.

[7] The time span investigated begins in 1970 because Germany did not have data on employment, TFP and average annual hours worked before that year.

Chapter 3
Econometric Methods

Abstract This chapter presents the methodology for the construction of the large battery of panel unit root and stationarity tests employed in the first part of the analysis, which explicitly allow for cross-sectional dependence. Smith et al. (J Appl Econometrics 19:147–170, 2004) and Hadri (Econom J 3:148–161, 2000) control for general forms of cross-dependence through bootstrap methods, Breitung and Das (Statistica Neerlandica 59:414–433, 2005) control for contemporaneous cross-correlation through seemingly-unrelated methods, Chang (J Econom 110:261–292, 2002) allows for cross-correlation by using a nonlinear instrumental variables method, Choi (Econometric theory and practice: frontiers of analysis and applied research: essays in honor of Peter C.B. Phillips, pp 311–334, 2002) considers a restrictive one-factor model in which all cross-sectional units are equally affected by the common factor, Pesaran (J Appl Econom 22(2):265–312, 2007) also allows for one common factor but with different factor loadings across units, and Moon and Perron (J Econom 122:81–126, 2004) and Harris et al. (J Bus Econ Stat 23:395–409, 2005) incorporate multiple common factors.

Keywords Panel unit root tests · Panel stationarity tests · Cross-sectional dependence · Bootstrap distribution · Factor models · Nonlinear instrumental variables

Having presented both the specification and data considered in the empirical analysis, we shift the focus to describe the methodology behind the different panel unit root and stationarity tests employed to determine the presence or absence of stochastic and deterministic convergence. Prior to that, we describe the methodology for the construction of the cross-sectional dependence test employed to determine whether our panels display cross-dependencies across panel members.

3.1 Test for Cross-Sectional Dependence in Panels

Pesaran (2004) develops a simple test of error cross-sectional dependence which is based on the average of pair-wise correlation coefficients of ordinary least squares (OLS) residuals obtained from standard ADF regressions for each individual.

M. Hernández Salmerón and D. Romero-Ávila, *Convergence in Output and Its Sources Among Industrialised Countries*,
SpringerBriefs in Economics, DOI 10.1007/978-3-319-13635-6_3

The order of the autoregressive model is selected using the *t-sig* criterion in Ng and Perron (1995), with the maximum number of lags set at $p = 4(T/100)^{1/4}$. Let $\hat{\rho}_{ij}$ be the sample estimate of the pair-wise correlation coefficient of OLS residuals:

$$\hat{\rho}_{ij} = \hat{\rho}_{ji} = \frac{\sum_{t=1}^{T} e_{it} e_{jt}}{\left(\sum_{t=1}^{T} e_{it}^2\right)^{1/2} \left(\sum_{t=1}^{T} e_{jt}^2\right)^{1/2}} \tag{3.1}$$

where e_{it} represents the OLS estimated residuals for individual i. On the basis of pair-wise correlation coefficients, Pesaran (2004) proposes a test of cross-sectional dependence with good finite-sample properties that does not depend on any particular spatial weight matrix, as occurs to the Breusch and Pagan (1980)'s LM test when N is large. Pesaran's cross-dependence statistic is defined by:

$$CD = \left[\frac{TN(N-1)}{2}\right]^{1/2} \bar{\hat{\rho}} \xrightarrow{d} N(0, 1) \tag{3.2}$$

where $\bar{\hat{\rho}} = \left(\frac{2}{N(N-1)}\right) \sum_{i=1}^{N-1} \sum_{j=i+1}^{N} \hat{\rho}_{ij}$, which represents the average of the correlation coefficients across all pairs. Under the null hypothesis of cross-sectional independence, the CD statistic is distributed as a two-tailed standard normal distribution and is general enough to account for the complicated dynamics of heterogeneous panels even in the case of a mix of stationary and nonstationary processes.

3.2 Panel Unit Root and Stationarity Tests with Cross-Sectional Dependence

3.2.1 Smith et al. (2004) Panel Unit Root Statistics

Smith et al. (2004) develop panel versions of some powerful modifications of the univariate ADF t-statistic such as the Max test of Leybourne (1995) and the weighted symmetric (WS) test of Pantula et al. (1994). Smith et al. (2004) consider a panel specification for the no-trend case applicable to the analysis of deterministic convergence such that:

$$\Delta y_{it} = \alpha_i + \gamma_i y_{it-1} + \sum_{j=2}^{p_i} \delta_{ij} \Delta y_{i,t-j-1} + \varepsilon_{it} \tag{3.3}$$

where p_i is the required degree of lag augmentation to make the residuals white noise, α_i represents the country-specific fixed effects, and $i = 1, \ldots, N$ and $t = 1, \ldots, T$ stand for the number of panel members and time periods, respectively. For the investigation of stochastic convergence, Eq. (3.3) would contain country-specific deterministic trends given by the term $\delta_i t$. To achieve the most parsimonious model compatible with white noise residuals, p_i is determined by the conventional step-down procedure of Ng and Perron (1995) setting a maximum lag order of 8. The first two tests are the standard Im et al. (2003)—IPS hereafter—tests. The t-bar statistic is computed as an average of individual t-statistics from ADF specifications, i.e. $\bar{t}_{NT} = N^{-1}\sum_{i=1}^{N} t_i$, where $i = 1, \ldots, N$ and $t = 1, \ldots, T$. The standardised statistic is given by:

$$\Psi_{\bar{t}} = \frac{\sqrt{N}(\bar{t}_{NT} - E(t_i))}{\sqrt{Var(t_i)}} \tag{3.4}$$

where $E(t_i)$ and $Var(t_i)$ are the expected value of the mean and variance, respectively. IPS also proposed the LM test statistic, which after normalisation takes the form:

$$\Psi_{LM} = \frac{\sqrt{N}(LM_{NT} - E(LM_i))}{\sqrt{Var(LM_i)}} \tag{3.5}$$

where LM_i is the individual LM test and $LM_{NT} = N^{-1}\sum_{i=1}^{N} LM_i$.

Leybourne (1995) proposed to obtain the ADF t-statistic from original data (DF_{fi}), and from time-reversed data $(z_{it} = y_{i,T+1-t})$ yielding DF_{ri}. The Max t-statistic for individual i is obtained as $\text{Max}_i = \text{Max}(DF_{fi}, DF_{ri})$. In a panel framework, the panel Max t-statistic takes the form:

$$\Psi_{\text{Max}} = \frac{\sqrt{N}(\text{Max}_{NT} - E(\text{Max}_i))}{\sqrt{Var(\text{Max}_i)}} \tag{3.6}$$

where $\text{Max}_{NT} = N^{-1}\sum_{i=1}^{N} \text{Max}_i$. Likewise, individual WS tests are computed as in Pantula et al. (1994), and the panel WS statistic is given by:

$$\Psi_{WS} = \frac{\sqrt{N}(WS_{NT} - E(WS_i))}{\sqrt{Var(WS_i)}} \tag{3.7}$$

where $WS_{NT} = N^{-1}\sum_{i=1}^{N} WS_i$ and WS_i is the univariate weighted symmetric statistic. Finally, Smith et al. (2004) present a more powerful variant of the LM statistic, which is computed on the basis of forward and reverse ADF regressions yielding the univariate LM_{fi} and LM_{ri}. Since both statistics take a positive value, the minimum LM statistic is computed as $\text{Min}_i = \text{Min}(LM_{fi}, LM_{ri})$. The panel statistic takes the form:

$$\Psi_{\mathrm{Min}} = \frac{\sqrt{N}(\mathrm{Min}_{NT} - E(\mathrm{Min}_i))}{\sqrt{Var(\mathrm{Min}_i)}} \tag{3.8}$$

where $\mathrm{Min}_{NT} = N^{-1}\sum_{i=1}^{N}\mathrm{Min}_i$. Since all of these tests assume both cross-sectional independence and asymptotic normality, Smith et al. (2004) develop a modified bootstrap procedure to compute p-values of the statistics which are robust to small-sample bias as well as to cross-sectional dependencies in the data.[1] $\Psi_{\bar{t}}$, Ψ_{Max} and Ψ_{WS} reject the null hypothesis for large negative values of the statistic, while Ψ_{LM} and Ψ_{Min} reject the null for large positive values.[2]

3.2.2 Breitung and Das (2005) Panel Unit Root Test

Breitung and Das (2005) consider a model like (3.3) while assuming the existence of weak cross-sectional dependence. For that purpose, they write the model as a seemingly unrelated-type (SUR) system of equations in matrix form[3]: $\Delta y_t = \phi y_{t-1} + \varepsilon_t$, where Δy_t, y_{t-1} and ε_t are $N \times 1$ vectors. The cross-sectional correlation is represented by a non-diagonal covariance matrix $\Omega = E(\varepsilon_t \varepsilon_t')$ for all t, with bounded eigenvalues. Breitung and Das (2005) demean the data such that $\tilde{y}_t = y_t - y_0$, where y_0 represents the value of the initial observation, and estimate consistently the variance-covariance matrix of the OLS estimator, which is denoted by $\hat{\upsilon}_{\hat{\varphi}}$. They then obtain the robust t-statistic free of size distortions due to contemporaneous cross-sectional correlation for N and T tending to infinity:

$$t_{rob} = \frac{\hat{\phi}}{\sqrt{\hat{\upsilon}_{\hat{\varphi}}}} = \frac{\sum_{t=1}^{T}\tilde{y}_{t-1}'\Delta\tilde{y}_t}{\sqrt{\sum_{t=1}^{T}\tilde{y}_{t-1}'\hat{\Omega}\tilde{y}_{t-1}}} \xrightarrow{d} N(0,1) \tag{3.9}$$

3.2.3 Chang (2002) Panel Unit Root Tests

Chang (2002) develops a group-mean unit root test based on a nonlinear IV estimation method. In a first step, she estimates the autoregressive coefficient from a standard ADF regression for each cross-sectional unit. In order to allow for cross-sectional

---

[1] See Smith et al. (2004, pp. 165–166) for details on the bootstrap procedure in a similar spirit to that in Maddala and Wu (1999). This method generates bootstrap innovations through resampling using a block size of 30 and 20,000 replications. The maximum lag order of autocorrelation used to compute the statistics is set at 8.

[2] All the five tests take the presence of a unit root for all individuals as the null hypothesis vs. the alternative hypothesis of stationarity for at least one individual unit.

[3] For expositional simplicity we abstract from lagged augmented terms.

dependence, Chang employs the instruments generated by a nonlinear function which constitutes a nonlinear transformation of the lagged values of the endogenous variable given by $F(y_{i,t-1})$. This function $F(\cdot)$ is called the instrument generating function (IGF hereafter) and must provide instruments which are strongly correlated with the regressor $y_{i,t-1}$. In a second step, Chang constructs the individual t-statistic for each unit (Z_i), which can then be used for testing the unit root null based on the nonlinear estimator. These t-statistics have a limiting standard distribution, and the asymptotic distributions of individual Z_i statistics are independent across units.[4] Therefore, in a third step, Chang proposes an average IV t-statistic, which has a standard limiting distribution:

$$S_N = \frac{1}{\sqrt{N}} \sum_{i=1}^{N} Z_i \xrightarrow{d} N(0,1) \tag{3.10}$$

Chang finds from simulations that the IV nonlinear panel unit root test outperforms the IPS test in terms of size and power. The value of the S_N statistic must be compared with the critical values from the lower tail of a standard normal distribution. In our application, we consider three examples of regularly integrated IGFs. The first is given by $IGF_1(x) = x \cdot \exp(-c_i|x|)$ where $c_i \in \Re$, $c_i = 3T^{-1/2}s^{-1}(\Delta y_{it})$ and $s^2(\Delta y_{it})$ is the sample standard error of Δy_{it}. In addition, we use $IGF_2(x) = \mathrm{I}(|x| < K)$—where K is a truncation parameter and the IV estimator obtained from IGF_2 is the trimmed OLS estimator based on the observations located in the interval $[-K, K]$—and $IGF_3(x) = \mathrm{I}(|x| < K) \cdot x$.

3.2.4 Hadri (2000) Panel Stationarity Statistic

Hadri (2000) develops a panel stationarity test which is robust to the presence of autocorrelated and heteroskedastic errors. Let $\{y_{i,t}\}$ be the set of stochastic processes given by:

$$y_{i,t} = \alpha_{i,t} + \beta_i t + \varepsilon_{i,t} \text{ and } \alpha_{i,t} = \alpha_{i,t-1} + \upsilon_{i,t} \tag{3.11}$$

where $\alpha_{i,t}$ is a random walk, $\upsilon_{i,t}$ is *i.d.d.* $(0, \sigma^2_\upsilon)$ and $\{\varepsilon_{i,t}\}$ and $\{\upsilon_{i,t}\}$ are assumed mutually independent. The null hypothesis of stationarity implies that $\alpha_{i,t}$ collapses into a constant ($\sigma^2_{\upsilon,i} = 0$ for all i) versus the alternative hypothesis that $\sigma^2_{\upsilon,i} > 0$ for

[4] Asymptotic independence of individual t-statistics is achieved by establishing asymptotic orthogonalities of the nonlinear instruments used in the construction of individual IV t-statistics. As a result, in a panel setting, one does not need to impose independence across units or to rely on sequential asymptotics in order to be able to construct panel unit root tests based on averaging across individual statistics.

some i, consistent with a unit root in those series. Hadri (2000) computes the panel stationarity test as the average of univariate KPSS tests:

$$\eta_k = N^{-1} \sum_{i=1}^{N} \left(\hat{\sigma}_i^{-2} T^{-2} \sum_{t=1}^{T} \hat{S}_{i,t}^2 \right), \tag{3.12}$$

where $\hat{\sigma}_i^{-2} T^{-2} \sum_{t=1}^{T} \hat{S}_{i,t}^2 = \eta_i$ is the univariate KPSS test for individual i, and $\hat{S}_{i,t} = \sum_{j=1}^{t} \hat{\varepsilon}_{i,j}$ stands for the partial sum of the estimated OLS residuals from (3.11). $\hat{\sigma}_i^2$ represents a consistent estimate of the long-run variance of $\varepsilon_{i,t}$, which allows for serial correlation and heteroskedasticity across the cross-sectional dimension.[5] Equation (3.12) allows for heterogeneity in the estimation of the long-run variances across units, but homogeneity can also be assumed by replacing $\hat{\sigma}_i^2$ in (3.12) with $\hat{\sigma}^2 = N^{-1} \sum_{i=1}^{N} \hat{\sigma}_i^2$. For the sake of robustness, we compute the panel stationarity test under both assumptions. After standardising the test, we have

$$LM = \frac{\sqrt{N}(\eta_k - \mu)}{v} \xrightarrow{d} N(0, 1) \tag{3.13}$$

where μ and v^2 are the mean and variance adjustment factors such that $\mu = 1/6$ and $v^2 = 1/45$ for the specification without trends and $\mu = 1/15$ and $v^2 = 11/6{,}300$ for the specification with trends.[6] The computation of Hadri's statistic requires the individual series to be cross-sectionally independent along with asymptotic normality. Since these assumptions are unlikely to hold in practice, we will compute the bootstrap distribution of the panel stationarity test following Maddala and Wu (1999) to allow for general forms of cross-sectional dependence, thereby correcting for finite-sample bias.

3.2.5 Choi (2002) Panel Unit Root Tests

Choi (2002) considers a restricted factor model in that all cross-sectional units are equally affected by the common factor. Choi eliminates cross-sectional correlations and deterministic components using GLS detrending methods and cross-sectional demeaning for panel data. His model is

$$\begin{aligned} u_{it} &= \alpha_i + f_t + \varepsilon_{it} \\ \varepsilon_{it} &= \sum_{j=1}^{q_i} d_{i,j} \varepsilon_{i,t-j} + v_{it} \end{aligned} \tag{3.14}$$

---

[5] These are obtained non-parametrically using the Quadratic Spectral kernel with fixed bandwidth.

[6] Hadri's statistic must be compared with the upper tail of the standard normal distribution.

where v_{it} are i.d.d $(0, \sigma^2_{v,i})$ and assumed to be cross-sectionally independent. α_i and f_t stand for the unobservable individual and time effects, respectively. For model (3.14), the null hypothesis implies the presence of a unit root in the remaining random component ε_{it}, i.e. $\sum_{i=1}^{q_i} d_{i,j} = 1$ for all i, versus the alternative hypothesis that $\sum_{i=1}^{q_i} d_{i,j} < 1$ for some i (i.e., stationarity for some i). From ADF regressions with the cross-sectionally independent transformed variables, Choi (2002) obtains the p-values used to construct the three panel combination tests of Choi (2001) but for the case of cross-sectionally dependent panels. We next outline the three statistics developed by Choi (2001), who followed Maddala and Wu (1999) by combining p-values from individual unit root tests in order to formulate panel unit root tests. He proposed three Fisher-type statistics for $T \to \infty$ and then $N \to \infty$. First, the modified inverse Chi-square test

$$P_m = -\frac{1}{\sqrt{N}}\sum_{i=1}^{N}(Ln(p_i) + 1) \xrightarrow{d} N(0, 1) \tag{3.15}$$

Second, the inverse normal test

$$Z = \frac{1}{\sqrt{N}}\sum_{i=1}^{N}\Phi^{-1}(p_i) \xrightarrow{d} N(0, 1) \tag{3.16}$$

Where $\Phi^{-1}(p_i)$ is a standard normal cumulative distribution function since $0 \leq p_i \leq 1$. Third, the modified logit test[7]

$$L^* = \frac{1}{\sqrt{\pi^2 N/3}}\sum_{i=1}^{N} Ln\left(\frac{p_i}{1 - p_i}\right) \xrightarrow{d} N(0, 1) \tag{3.17}$$

3.2.6 *Moon and Perron (2004) Panel Unit Root Statistics*

Moon and Perron (2004) develop two panel unit root tests which allow for cross-sectional dependence through an approximate linear dynamic factor model. The main difference with respect to the factor model of Bai and Ng (2004a) is that the common factors are unobservable and thus included in the error term. These factors are common across cross-sectional units but with heterogeneous intensity. To estimate the factor loadings, they employ the principal components method and the number of common factors is determined using the information criteria developed by Bai and Ng (2002), which include the IC_p and BIC_3 criteria used in the next

---

[7] P_m must be compared with the critical values from the upper tail of the standard normal distribution, and Z and L^* with the critical values from the lower tail of the standard normal distribution.

chapter in the computation of the Bai and Ng (2004a) unit root tests. The estimation and testing procedures are based on the de-factored data which are obtained by a projection onto the space orthogonal to the factor loadings. Thus, defactored data no longer exhibit cross-dependence. Under the null, the two panel unit root tests follow a standard normal distribution for T and N tending to infinity[8]:

$$t_a = \frac{\sqrt{N}T(\hat{\rho}^+_{pool} - 1)}{\sqrt{\frac{2\hat{\phi}^4_e}{\hat{\omega}^4_e}}} \xrightarrow{d} N(0,1) \tag{3.18}$$

$$t_b = \sqrt{N}T(\hat{\rho}^+_{pool} - 1)\sqrt{\frac{1}{NT^2} trace(Y_{-1}Q_\Lambda Y'_{-1})}\frac{\hat{\omega}^2_e}{\hat{\phi}^4_e} \xrightarrow{d} N(0,1) \tag{3.19}$$

where $\hat{\rho}^+_{pool}$ is the bias-corrected OLS estimate of the pooled autoregressive parameter obtained with the defactored panel data, Y is the matrix of the observations on y_{it}, Y_{-1} is the matrix of the corresponding lagged values and Q_Λ is the projection matrix used to eliminate the common factors. The term $\hat{\omega}^2_e$ is computed as a cross-sectional average of $\hat{\omega}^2_{e,i}$, i.e. the long-run variance of the estimated residuals $\hat{e}_{it}$,[9] and $\hat{\phi}^4_e$ as the cross-sectional average of $\hat{\omega}^4_{e,i}$.

3.2.7 Pesaran (2007) Panel Unit Root Statistics

Pesaran (2007) models cross-sectional correlation using a one-factor model given by $u_{it} = \gamma_i f_t + \varepsilon_{it}$, where f_t is the unobserved common factor, γ_i is the factor loading coefficient and ε_{it} is the idiosyncratic error component. Pesaran augments standard ADF specifications with the cross-sectional averages of lagged levels and first-differences of the series in order to eliminate the cross-sectional dependence embodied in $\gamma_i f_t$. This is done as follows for the no-trend specification with no serial correlation in the error:

$$\Delta y_{it} = \alpha_i + \rho_i y_{it-1} + c_i \bar{y}_{t-1} + d_i \Delta\bar{y} + \upsilon_{it} \tag{3.20}$$

---

[8] The panel unit root tests of Moon and Perron (2004) take the null hypothesis of nonstationarity for all cross-sectional units, versus the alternative of stationarity for all units. In contrast, the tests of Chang (2002), Choi (2002), Smith et al. (2004), Breitung and Das (2005) and Pesaran (2007) described in this chapter and Bai and Ng (2004a) employed in chapter 5, all take the null hypothesis of nonstationarity for all units, versus the alternative hypothesis of stationarity for at least one unit.

[9] The long-run variance of the residuals is computed with both the Barlett and Quadratic Spectral kernels with non-parametric Newey-West (1994) bandwidth selection. As a result, we present two sets of Moon and Perron (2004) statistics.

where $\bar{y}_{t-1} = (1/N)\sum_{i=1}^{N} y_{it-1}$ and $\Delta\bar{y}_t = (1/N)\sum_{i=1}^{N} \Delta y_{it}$. In the case of serially correlated residuals, the cross-sectionally augmented specification would incorporate $\Delta\bar{y}_{t-j}$ and Δy_{it-j} terms for $j = 1, \ldots, p$. Pesaran then computes cross-sectionally augmented ADF t-statistics, i.e. $CADF_i$ for each i associated with the OLS estimate of ρ_i, which are denoted by $t_i(N, T)$. A truncated version ($CADF_i^*$) is also considered to correct for undue influence of extreme observations in short-T panels. Pesaran (2007) constructs a modified version of the IPS t-bar test by averaging individual $CADF_i$ and $CADF_i^*$ statistics, rendering the cross-sectionally augmented IPS statistics, i.e. $CIPS = N^{-1}\sum_{i=1}^{N} t_i(N, T)$ and $CIPS^* = N^{-1}\sum_{i=1}^{N} t_i^*(N, T)$, with $t_i^*(N, T)$ denoting the truncated $CADF$ statistic. In addition, Pesaran combines p-values of $CADF_i$ to compute the inverse Chi-square test statistic $CP = -2\sum_{i=1}^{N}\ln(p_{iT})$ and the inverse normal test $CZ = N^{-1/2}\sum_{i=1}^{N}\Phi^{-1}(p_{iT})$, where p_{iT} is the p-value associated with $CADF_i$. In the presence of cross-sectional dependence, these statistics no longer follow standard distributions and the critical values must be simulated for various sample sizes.

3.2.8 Harris et al. (2005) Panel Stationarity Statistic

Harris et al. (2005) propose a panel stationarity test that is able to handle time-series and cross-sectional dynamics, thereby allowing for heterogeneity in the deterministics across units. This test addresses cross-sectional dependence through a factor model with an unknown number of factors like:

$$\begin{aligned} y_{it} &= \beta_i' x_{it} + z_{it} \\ z_{it} &= \lambda_i' f_t + e_{it} \end{aligned} \tag{3.21}$$

where f_t is an $r \times 1$ vector of latent factors which needs to be estimated to determine the rank, λ_i is an $r \times 1$ vector of loading parameters and e_{it} is the idiosyncratic term for each i. They further assume that f_t and e_{it} are mutually independent of one another. They present a specification that contains a constant but not a trend. The authors compute the number of common factors by minimising the IC_1 method proposed by Bai and Ng (2002), setting the maximum number of factors to 5. They then compute the $\hat{S}_k^F$ test for the estimated components $\hat{f}_t$ and $\hat{e}_{it}$ jointly, which is robust to cross-sectional correlation and serves as a test for the null hypothesis that the series z_{it} are stationary for all i.[10] More specifically, the resulting statistic takes the form:

[10] The null hypothesis implies that all cross-sectional units are stationary against the alternative that at least one unit is nonstationary.

$$\hat{S}_k^F = \frac{\tilde{C}_k}{\hat{\omega}\{\tilde{a}_{k,t}\}} \xrightarrow{d} N(0,1) \tag{3.22}$$

where $\hat{\omega}^2\{\tilde{a}_{k,t}\}$ is the long-run variance estimator, $\tilde{C}_k = T^{-1/2}\sum_{t=k+1}^{T}\tilde{a}_{k,t}$, $\tilde{a}_{k,t} = \sum_{i=1}^{N}\tilde{z}_{it}\tilde{z}_{it-k}$, $\tilde{z}_{it}$ are standardised residuals and $k = (3T)^{1/2}$. The long-run variance is estimated with the Bartlett lag window with $l = \left[12(T/10)^{1/4}\right]$. It can be shown that $\hat{S}_k^F$ follows a standard normal distribution even when it is based on residuals with large T and fixed N.

Chapter 4
Empirical Results

Abstract This chapter investigates the existence of stochastic and deterministic convergence of real output per worker and the sources of output (physical capital per worker, human capital per worker, total factor productivity and average annual hours worked) in 21 OECD countries over the period 1970–2011. Towards this end, we apply a large battery of panel unit root and stationarity tests, all robust to the presence of cross-sectional dependence. The analysis fails to provide clear-cut evidence of convergence dynamics either in real GDP per worker or in the series of the sources of output. Except for the panel unit root tests of Choi (2002) and Moon and Perron (2004), the panel unit root statistics of Chang (2002), Smith et al. (2004), Breitung and Das (2005) and Pesaran (2007) as well as the panel stationarity tests of Hadri (2000) and Harris et al. (2005) do not generally support the convergence hypothesis.

Keywords Stochastic convergence · Deterministic convergence · Panel unit root testing · Cross-sectional dependence

4.1 Initial Results Regarding σ-Convergence

As a preliminary check, we depict the log of real output per worker, real physical capital per worker, human capital, TFP and average annual hours worked. These are shown in Figs. 4.1, 4.2, 4.3, 4.4 and 4.5, respectively. It is worth noting that there does not appear to be a clear narrowing of cross-country differences in real GDP per worker, thus failing to show a tendency for the dispersion in this series to decrease over the period 1970–2011. Instead, Fig. 4.1 shows a rather stable pattern among the series of log real GDP per worker. A similar picture is provided for the log of real physical capital per worker (Fig. 4.2), human capital (Fig. 4.3), and average annual hours worked (Fig. 4.5). Only Fig. 4.4, for the case of the log of relative TFP, does show a narrowing of TFP differences among OECD countries over the period 1970–2011.

M. Hernández Salmerón and D. Romero-Ávila, *Convergence in Output and Its Sources Among Industrialised Countries*,
SpringerBriefs in Economics, DOI 10.1007/978-3-319-13635-6_4

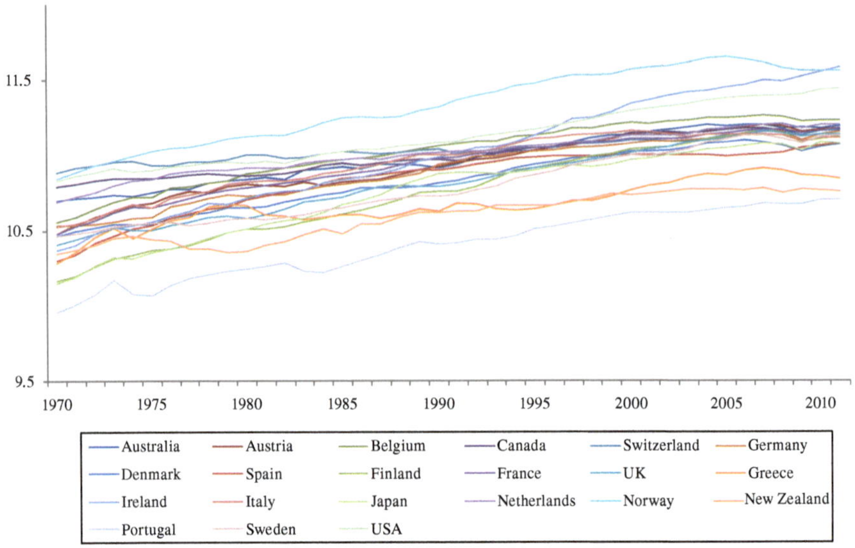

Fig. 4.1 Log real GDP per worker

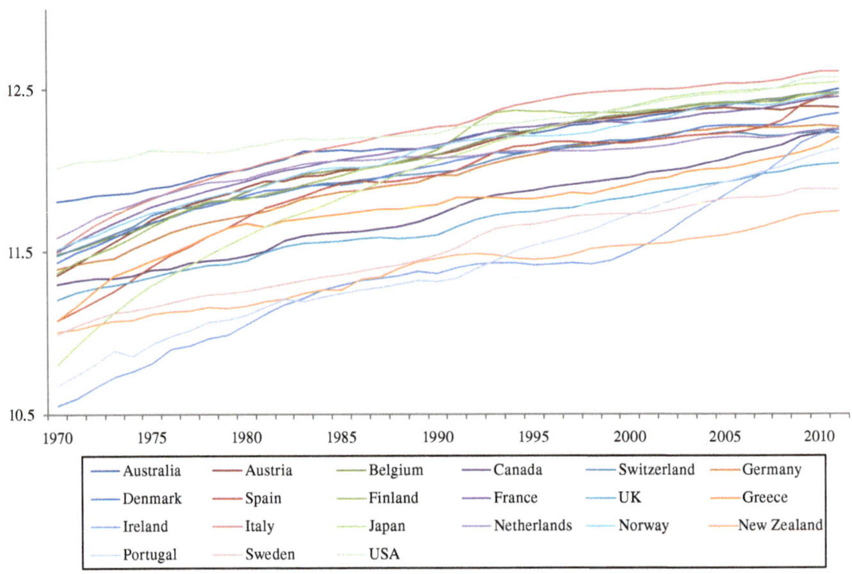

Fig. 4.2 Log real physical capital per worker

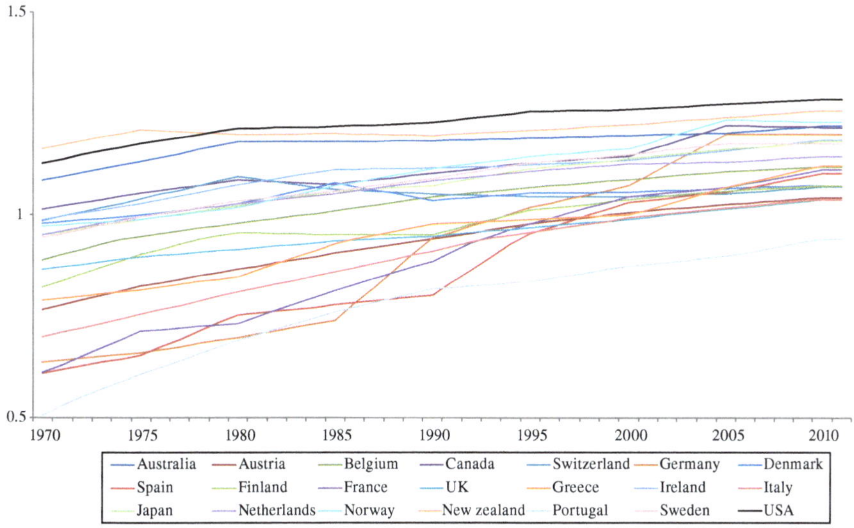

Fig. 4.3 Log human capital index

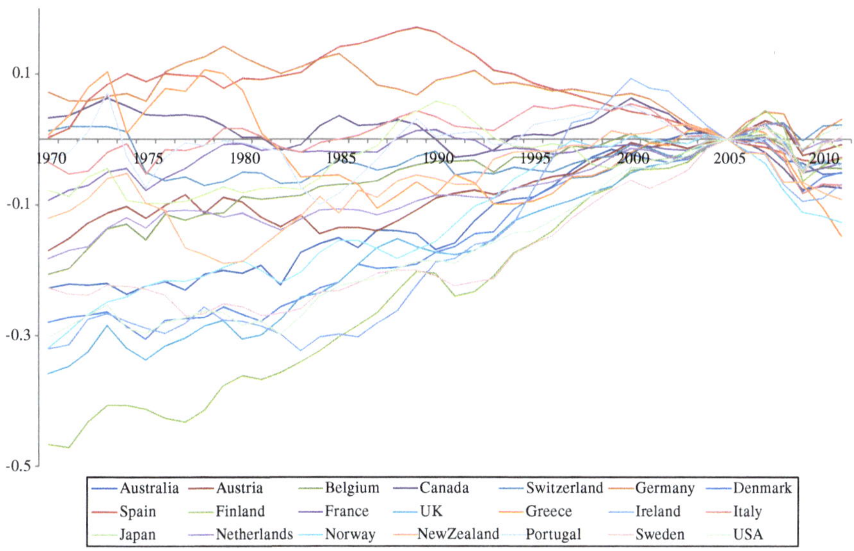

Fig. 4.4 Log total factor productivity

In Figs. 4.6, 4.7, 4.8, 4.9 and 4.10, we plot the standard deviation of the natural log of relative real output per worker and the output sources variables. Figure 4.6 shows a fall in the standard deviation of the natural logarithm of relative GDP per worker from about 24.5 % in 1970 to 18.7 % in 1990, but from that point in time the

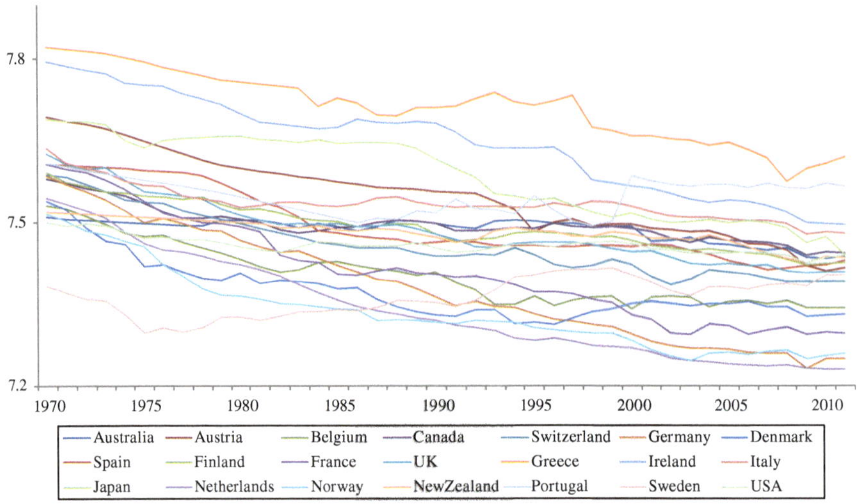

Fig. 4.5 Log annual average hours

standard deviation begins to rise up to a value of 21.5 % in 2011. Therefore, over the whole period there is a slight fall in dispersion supporting the σ-convergence hypothesis, which indicates the existence of a minor tendency for cross-country output per worker differences to decline over the past four decades. Regarding the sources of output per worker, Figs. 4.7, 4.8 and 4.9 show a clear tendency for cross-country differences in real physical capital per worker, human capital and TFP to fall. As a matter of fact, the standard deviation has fallen from 35.6 to 22.5 % between

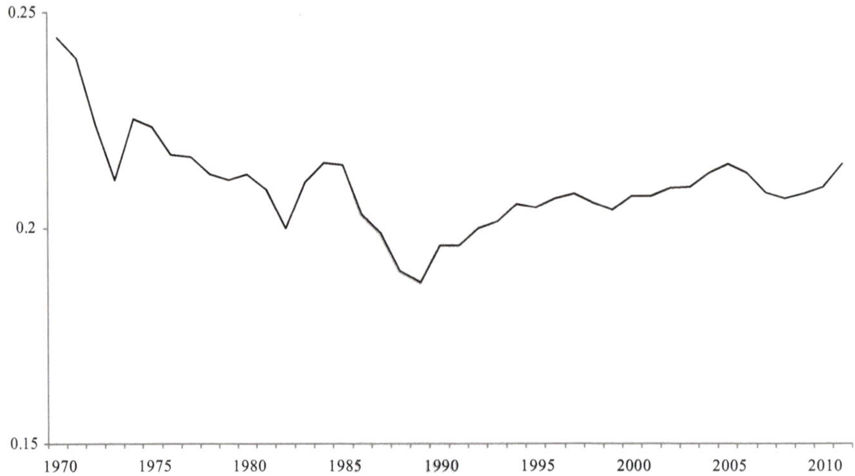

Fig. 4.6 σ-convergence: real GDP per worker

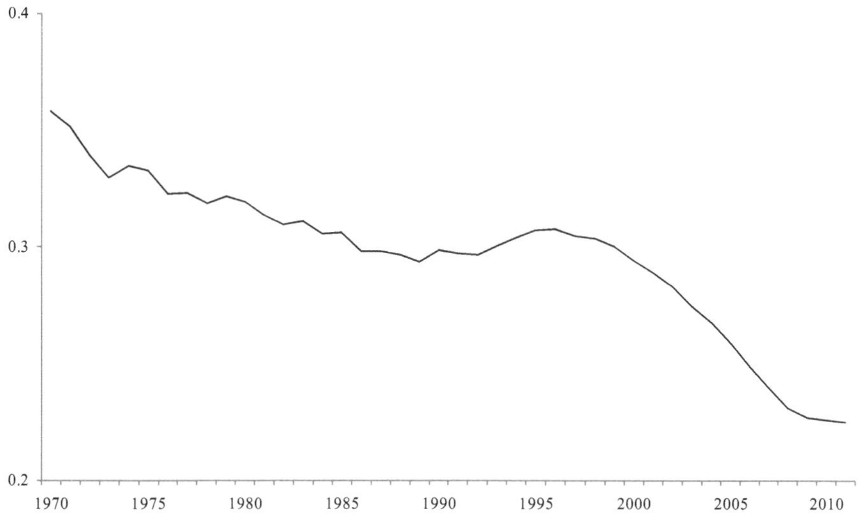

Fig. 4.7 σ-convergence: real physical capital per worker

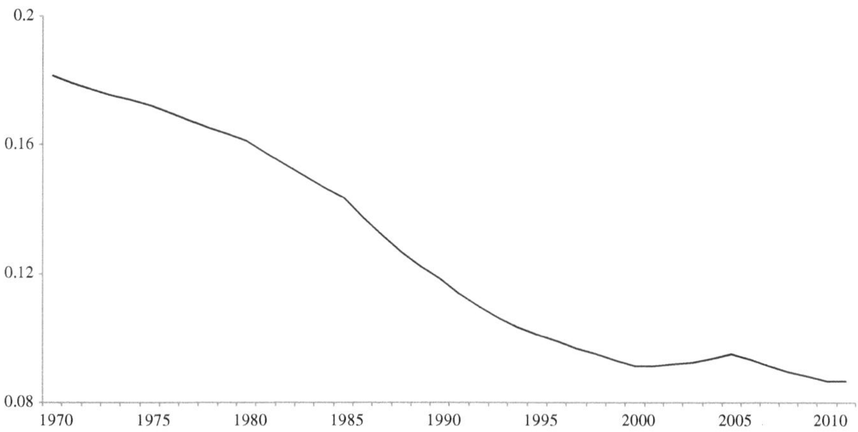

Fig. 4.8 σ-convergence: human capital index

1970 and 2011 for real physical capital per worker, from 18.2 to 8.6 % for the human capital index, and from about 15 to 4.6 % for TFP. As regards average annual hours worked, despite exhibiting some cyclical fluctuations, the standard deviation of the series remains fairly constant between 1970 and 2011 at around 10 %.

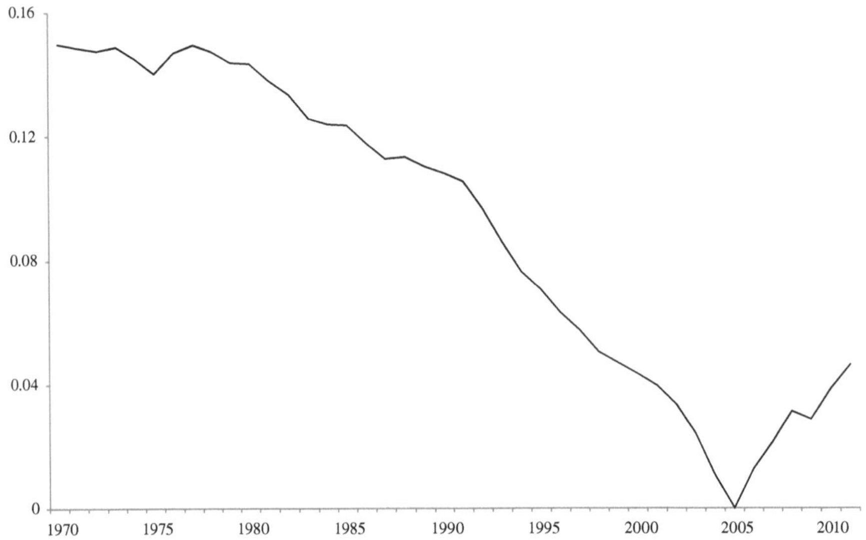

Fig. 4.9 σ-convergence: total factor productivity

Fig. 4.10 σ-convergence: annual average hours

4.2 Results Regarding Cross-Sectional Dependence

We exploit the time-series and cross-section dimensions of the data because it is widely recognised in the literature that the use of panel unit root and stationarity tests that exploit the cross-sectional variation of the data leads to a much more

Table 4.1 Cross-sectional dependence test

	Real GDP per worker	Real physical capital per worker	Human capital index	Total factor productivity	Annual average hours
Trend specification: stochastic convergence					
CD test	21.115***	20.369***	19.442***	29.597***	9.030***
p-value	0.000	0.000	0.000	0.000	0.000
No trend specification: deterministic convergence					
CD test	23.475***	18.656***	18.147***	31.438***	8.698***
p-value	0.000	0.000	0.000	0.000	0.000

The CD-statistic tests for the null of cross-sectional independence and is distributed as a two-tailed standard normal distribution

*** implies rejection of the null hypothesis at the 1 % significance level

efficient way to achieve substantial power gains. However, one important caveat applies when conducting panel unit root testing: traditional panel unit root and stationarity tests derived under the assumption of cross-sectional independence are subject to severe size distortions, which leads to spuriously over-reject the null hypothesis (O'Connell 1998; Maddala and Wu 1999; Strauss and Yigit 2003; Banerjee et al. 2005). As the international real business cycle literature has demonstrated, there are strong linkages between macroeconomic aggregates among industrialised countries (see Backus et al. 1992; Devereux et al. 1992). As a result, we explicitly allow for cross-sectional dependence in all the panel unit root and stationarity tests employed in the analysis.

In order to make sure that cross-sectional dependence is actually present in our panels of real output per worker, real physical capital per worker, human capital, TFP and average annual hours worked, we begin the analysis by applying the CD statistic of Pesaran (2004) to innovations in the respective series for the panel of 21 OECD countries over the period 1970–2011. For each unit i we compute OLS residuals from ADF regressions like (3.3), where the optimal lag-order is determined using the general-to-specific procedure suggested by Ng and Perron (1995) with a maximum lag-order of $p = 4(T/100)^{1/4}$. As reported in Table 4.1, the null hypothesis that innovations in the respective series are cross-sectionally independent is strongly rejected for all of the five variables analysed. This result is robust to the inclusion of a linear trend in the specification.[1] Therefore, it is necessary to allow for cross-correlation in the analysis of stochastic and deterministic convergence. This finding seems plausible and accords well with the fact that

[1] Note that we apply the CD test to the panels of log real output per worker, log real physical capital per worker, log human capital, log TFP and log average annual hours worked, instead of applying it to the log of the respective relative series, which by assumption would exhibit cross-sectional dependence driven by the implicit cross-sectional demeaning.

industrialised countries are highly integrated in economic terms. This demonstrates that inferences deriving from the application of traditional panel unit root tests, which are computed under the assumption of error cross-sectional independence, are likely to be misleading as they are subject to dramatic size distortions.

4.3 Analysis of Stochastic Convergence

Having determined the prevalence of cross-sectional dependence in the panels of log relative real GDP per worker and its sources, we now move to investigate the existence of stochastic convergence through the application of a large battery of panel unit root and stationarity tests robust to cross-sectional dependence in the error structure of the panels studied. In reporting the results, we begin with the findings for the log of relative real GDP per worker, and then proceed with the results for the log of relative real physical capital per worker, human capital, TFP and average annual hours worked. The value of the panel statistic and the associated p-value for the panel unit root tests of Smith et al. (2004), Chang (2002), Breitung and Das (2005), Choi (2002), Moon and Perron (2004) and Pesaran (2007) and the panel stationarity test of Harris et al. (2005) are all presented in a single table for each respective variable (see Tables 4.2, 4.4, 4.6, 4.8 and 4.10). In addition, Hadri's statistic and associated p-value for the case of cross-sectional independence and asymptotic normality as well as the bootstrap critical values controlling for cross-correlation and finite-sample bias are all presented in another individual table for each respective series (see Tables 4.3, 4.5, 4.7, 4.9 and 4.11). In the left part of Tables 4.2, 4.4, 4.6, 4.8 and 4.10, we report the results associated with the weaker notion of convergence given by stochastic convergence. Likewise, in the right part of each table we report the results for the no-trend specification related to the stronger notion of deterministic convergence. Regarding Tables 4.3, 4.5, 4.7, 4.9 and 4.11 that report the results of Hadri's statistic, the left part of each table focuses on the trend specification containing the results of stochastic convergence, whereas the right part relates to the no-trend specification associated with deterministic convergence. Therefore, we begin the analysis by testing for the weaker notion of stochastic convergence, which is followed by the investigation of the stronger notion of deterministic convergence.

4.3.1 Convergence in Real GDP per Worker

We start with the results from the powerful unit root tests of Smith et al. (2004), which control for cross-dependence and for finite-sample bias through modified residual-based bootstrap methods. In deriving the empirical distributions of the five statistics tailored to the structure of the cross-sectional correlation of the error and to

Table 4.2 Panel unit root and stationarity tests: real GDP per worker

	Trend specification: stochastic convergence		No trend specification: deterministic convergence	
	Statistic	p-value	Statistic	p-value
Smith et al. (2004)				
$\Psi_{\bar{t}}$	−1.969	0.593	−1.679	0.130
Ψ_{Max}	−1.052	0.986	−0.567	0.879
Ψ_{LM}	4.626	0.506	4.494*	0.084
Ψ_{Min}	3.531	0.276	3.064**	0.032
Ψ_{WS}	−1.812	0.899	−0.874	0.851
Chang (2002)				
S_{N1}	−0.720	0.236	3.192	0.999
S_{N2}	−1.191	0.117	4.714	1.000
S_{N3}	0.406	0.658	3.519	1.000
Breitung and Das (2005)				
t_{rob}	0.256	0.601	−0.174	0.431
Choi (2002)				
Modified inverse chi-square test (Pm)	1.714**	0.043	6.553***	0.000
Inverse normal test (Z)	0.809	0.791	−4.008***	0.000
Modified logit test (L^*)	0.785	0.784	−4.633***	0.000
Moon and Perron (2004)				
t_a^* (Quadratic spectral kernel)	−1.966**	0.025	−5.970***	0.000
t_b^* (Quadratic spectral kernel)	−2.223**	0.013	−4.443***	0.000
t_a^* (Bartlett kernel)	−1.995**	0.023	−5.912***	0.000
t_b^* (Bartlett kernel)	−2.280**	0.011	−4.483***	0.000
Pesaran (2007)				
CIPS	−2.352	0.455	−1.329	0.950
*CIPS**	−2.352	0.455	−1.329	0.950
Optimal lag truncation	2		3	
CP	53.210		31.699	
CZ	−0.131		1.844	
Harris et al. (2005)				
$\hat{S}_k^F$			1.919**	0.028
No. factors (IC_1)			5	

Notes The bootstrap p-values for the five panel unit root tests of Smith et al. (2004) are computed employing 20,000 bootstrap replications and defining a block size equal to 30. The maximum lag order is set to 8. A general-to-specific procedure has been used to select the optimal lag-length. For the Moon and Perron (2004) and Harris et al. (2005) statistics we set the maximum number of factors to 5. The 1, 5 and 10 % critical values for the *CP* test (*CZ* test) are 78.49, 65.57 and 58.64 (−3.07, −2.23 and −1.75) for the specification without trends. The 1, 5 and 10 % critical values for the *CP* test (*CZ* test) are 78.90, 65.01 and 58.60 (−2.90, −2.05 and −1.59) for the specification with trends. These critical values are computed for T = 50 and N = 20. The $\hat{S}_k^F$ statistic is a panel stationarity test and the others are panel unit root tests

***, ** and * imply rejection of the null hypothesis at 1, 5 and 10 %, respectively

Table 4.3 Panel stationarity test of Hadri (2000): real GDP per worker

	Trend specification: stochastic convergence		No trend specification: deterministic convergence	
Panel A: panel KPSS test assuming cross-sectional independence				
	Test	*p*-value	Test	*p*-value
LM (Homogeneous)	8.889***	0.000	11.600***	0.000
LM (Heterogeneous)	7.421***	0.000	6.937***	0.000

Panel B: bootstrap critical values (assuming cross-section dependence)								
	10 %	5 %	2.5 %	1 %	10 %	5 %	2.5 %	1 %
LM (Homogeneous)	3.94	5.452	6.948	8.929	4.417	6.883	9.158	11.706
LM (Heterogeneous)	3.294	4.542	5.704	7.198	3.172	4.621	5.893	7.563

Notes The bootstrap critical values for Hadri's test are computed employing 20,000 bootstrap replications. LM (Homogeneous) and LM (Heterogeneous) denote the panel KPSS test of Hadri (2000) for the case of homogeneity and heterogeneity in the estimation of the long-run variance, respectively. The Spectral Quadratic kernel was employed

***, ** and * imply rejection of the null hypothesis at 1, 5 and 10 %, respectively

the sample size of our five panels, we employ a block size of 30 and 20,000 bootstrap replications. The maximum lag-order for individual specifications is set at eight. As reported in Table 4.2, none of the five statistics of Smith et al. (2004) renders statistically significant bootstrap *p*-values (at the 10 % level or lower) for the specification with trends associated with the concept of stochastic convergence.

As regards the nonlinear IV panel unit root tests of Chang (2002), our results remain fairly unchanged, since we clearly fail to reject the null of joint nonstationarity with any of the regularly integrated *IGFs* employed in the analysis.[2] Likewise, the Breitung and Das (2005) test, which controls for contemporaneous cross-correlation through a SUR approach, fails to reject the unit root null hypothesis of lack of stochastic convergence. As regards the three combination panel statistics of Choi (2002), we only reject the null hypothesis of lack of stochastic convergence at conventional significance levels with the modified inverse Chi-square statistic. As far as Pesaran's (2007) tests are concerned, our results confirm the above results, as we fail to reject the null of nonstationarity with any of the four tests. It is only with the two pooled panel unit root tests of Moon and Perron (2004) that we are able to reject the joint nonstationarity null hypothesis, thus supporting the presence of stochastic convergence patterns in real GDP per worker across OECD economies over the past 40 years. This occurs irrespective of the use of the Quadratic Spectral kernel or the Bartlett kernel in estimating the long-run variance of the residuals.

[2] The nonlinear IV panel unit root test of Chang (2002) has been recently criticised by Im and Pesaran (2003) on the grounds that under strong forms of cross-correlation, Chang's test displays size distortions. This criticism may be alleviated to some extent in panels with large T relative to N, as occurs with our panels of 21 OECD countries over the period 1970–2011. Furthermore, even if size distortions existed, we fail to reject the joint unit root null, which reinforces the view that log relative real GDP per worker may be best described as nonstationary.

Table 4.4 Panel unit root and stationarity tests: real physical capital per worker

	Trend specification: stochastic convergence		No trend specification: deterministic convergence	
	Statistic	*p*-value	Statistic	*p*-value
Smith et al. (2004)				
$\Psi_{\bar{t}}$	−1.928	0.712	−1.729	0.121
Ψ_{Max}	−0.998	0.989	−0.252	0.986
Ψ_{LM}	4.104	0.829	4.897**	0.025
Ψ_{Min}	2.060	0.975	2.681*	0.086
Ψ_{WS}	−1.631	0.980	−0.816	0.877
Chang (2002)				
S_{N1}	0.395	0.654	2.065	0.981
S_{N2}	−0.925	0.178	4.270	1.000
S_{N3}	−0.442	0.329	3.395	1.000
Breitung and Das (2005)				
t_{rob}	0.791	0.785	−1.122	0.131
Choi (2002)				
Modified inverse chi-square test (Pm)	−0.473	0.682	4.861***	0.000
Inverse normal test (Z)	2.899	0.998	−3.509***	0.000
Modified logit test (L)*	3.694	1.000	−3.512***	0.000
Moon and Perron (2004)				
t_a^* (Quadratic spectral kernel)	0.143	0.557	−9.099***	0.000
t_b^* (Quadratic spectral kernel)	0.123	0.549	−4.613***	0.000
t_a^* (Bartlett kernel)	0.137	0.555	−9.124***	0.000
t_b^* (Bartlett kernel)	0.117	0.547	−4.653***	0.000
Pesaran (2007)				
CIPS	−2.139	0.785	−1.952	0.245
*CIPS**	−2.139	0.785	−1.952	0.245
Optimal lag truncation	3		2	
CP	37.036		57.393	
CZ	0.800		−0.920	
Harris et al. (2005)				
$\hat{S}_k^F$			1.586*	0.056
No. factors (IC_1)			5	

Notes The bootstrap *p*-values for the five panel unit root tests of Smith et al. (2004) are computed employing 20,000 bootstrap replications and defining a block size equal to 30. The maximum lag order is set to 8. A general-to-specific procedure has been used to select the optimal lag-length. For the Moon and Perron (2004) and Harris et al. (2005) statistics we set the maximum number of factors to 5. The 1, 5 and 10 % critical values for the *CP* test (*CZ* test) are 78.49, 65.57 and 58.64 (−3.07, −2.23 and −1.75) for the specification without trends. The 1, 5 and 10 % critical values for the *CP* test (*CZ* test) are 78.90, 65.01 and 58.60 (−2.90, −2.05 and −1.59) for the specification with trends. These critical values are computed for T = 50 and N = 20. The $\hat{S}_k^F$ statistic is a panel stationarity test and the others are panel unit root tests

***, ** and * imply rejection of the null hypothesis at 1, 5 and 10 %, respectively

Table 4.5 Panel stationarity test of Hadri (2000): real physical capital per worker

	Trend specification: stochastic convergence				No trend specification: deterministic convergence			
Panel A: panel KPSS test assuming cross-sectional independence								
	Test		*p*-value		Test		*p*-value	
LM (Homogeneous)	8.339***		0.000		11.454***		0.000	
LM (Heterogeneous)	7.452***		0.000		7.903***		0.000	
Panel B: bootstrap critical values (assuming cross-section dependence)								
	10 %	5 %	2.5 %	1 %	10 %	5 %	2.5 %	1 %
LM (Homogeneous)	4.198	5.765	7.243	9.035	4.27	6.434	8.587	11.602
LM (Heterogeneous)	3.613	4.914	6.054	7.611	3.275	4.821	6.394	8.435

Notes The bootstrap critical values for Hadri's test are computed employing 20,000 bootstrap replications. LM (Homogeneous) and LM (Heterogeneous) denote the panel KPSS test of Hadri (2000) for the case of homogeneity and heterogeneity in the estimation of the long-run variance, respectively. The Spectral Quadratic kernel was employed

***, ** and * imply rejection of the null hypothesis at 1, 5 and 10 %, respectively

Table 4.3 shows the results of the panel stationarity test of Hadri (2000). Panel A reports the results of the computation of the test under the assumption of cross-sectional independence and asymptotic normality, while Panel B reports the bootstrap critical values allowing for general forms of cross-sectional dependence, thereby correcting for finite-sample bias. Under the assumption of cross-sectional independence, Hadri's test strongly rejects the null of stationarity in favour of a unit root, irrespective of the assumption of homogeneity or heterogeneity in the computation of the long-run variance. To deal with the issue of cross-dependence, we compute the bootstrap distribution of Hadri's test, which appears to dramatically shift to the right of the upper tail of the standard normal distribution. But despite this sharp rise in the critical values, we are still able to reject the null at the 2.5 % significance level for the case of homogeneity in the estimation of the long-run variance and at the 1 % level for the heterogeneity case. This supports the existence of a unit root in the log of relative GDP per worker, which implies a lack of stochastic convergence in real output per worker.

In all, except for the Moon and Perron (2004) panel unit root tests and the modified inverse Chi-square test of Choi (2002), the other statistics, which are the majority, favoured the unit root hypothesis for relative real GDP per worker. This is tantamount to saying that there is a lack of stochastic convergence in real output per worker.

4.3.2 Convergence in the Sources of Output per Worker

Having presented the results from the application of the large array of panel unit root and stationarity tests to the log of relative real GDP per worker, we next do so for the four series constituting the sources of output, i.e., real physical capital per

Table 4.6 Panel unit root and stationarity tests: human capital index

	Trend specification: stochastic convergence		No trend specification: deterministic convergence	
	Statistic	*p*-value	Statistic	*p*-value
Smith et al. (2004)				
$\Psi_{\bar{t}}$	−2.254	0.176	−1.758	0.112
Ψ_{Max}	−1.702	0.104	−0.833	0.187
Ψ_{LM}	6.289*	0.052	4.380	0.223
Ψ_{Min}	3.982**	0.026	2.675	0.126
Ψ_{WS}	−2.488**	0.014	−1.237	0.150
Chang (2002)				
S_{N1}	−1.139	0.127	0.248	0.598
S_{N2}	−1.801	0.036	3.846	1.000
S_{N3}	0.396	0.654	2.672	0.996
Breitung and Das (2005)				
t_{rob}	−0.054	0.478	0.132	0.553
Choi (2002)				
Modified inverse chi-square test (Pm)	3.422***	0.000	3.668***	0.000
Inverse normal test (Z)	−1.782**	0.037	−3.366***	0.000
Modified logit test (L)*	−1.592*	0.056	−3.505***	0.000
Moon and Perron (2004)				
t_a^* (Quadratic spectral kernel)	−1.997**	0.023	−25.824***	0.000
t_b^* (Quadratic spectral kernel)	−1.238	0.108	−7.565***	0.000
t_a^* (Bartlett kernel)	−2.002**	0.023	−23.845***	0.000
t_b^* (Bartlett kernel)	−1.289*	0.099	−7.258***	0.000
Pesaran (2007)				
CIPS	−2.610	0.115	−2.115*	0.095
*CIPS**	−2.610	0.115	−2.115*	0.095
Optimal lag truncation	4		4	
CP	55.500		58.619	
CZ	−1.426		−1.717	
Harris et al. (2005)				
$\hat{S}_k^F$			−0.784	0.783
No. factors (IC_1)			5	

Notes The bootstrap *p*-values for the five panel unit root tests of Smith et al. (2004) are computed employing 20,000 bootstrap replications and defining a block size equal to 30. The maximum lag order is set to 8. A general-to-specific procedure has been used to select the optimal lag-length. For the Moon and Perron (2004) and Harris et al. (2005) statistics we set the maximum number of factors to 5. The 1, 5 and 10 % critical values for the *CP* test (*CZ* test) are 78.49, 65.57 and 58.64 (−3.07, −2.23 and −1.75) for the specification without trends. The 1, 5 and 10 % critical values for the *CP* test (*CZ* test) are 78.90, 65.01 and 58.60 (−2.90, −2.05 and −1.59) for the specification with trends. These critical values are computed for T = 50 and N = 20. The $\hat{S}_k^F$ statistic is a panel stationarity test and the others are panel unit root tests
***, ** and * imply rejection of the null hypothesis at 1, 5 and 10 %, respectively

Table 4.7 Panel stationarity test of Hadri (2000): human capital index

	Trend specification: stochastic convergence				No trend specification: deterministic convergence			
Panel A: panel KPSS test assuming cross-sectional independence								
	Test		*p*-value		Test		*p*-value	
LM (Homogeneous)	5.184***		0.000		13.132***		0.000	
LM (Heterogeneous)	6.029***		0.000		11.141***		0.000	
Panel B: bootstrap critical values (assuming cross-section dependence)								
	10 %	5 %	2.5 %	1 %	10 %	5 %	2.5 %	1 %
LM (Homogeneous)	3.909	5.213	6.465	8.113	5.13	7.974	10.851	14.223
LM (Heterogeneous)	3.376	4.398	5.403	6.64	4.197	6.492	8.704	11.499

Notes The bootstrap critical values for Hadri's test are computed employing 20,000 bootstrap replications. LM (Homogeneous) and LM (Heterogeneous) denote the panel KPSS test of Hadri (2000) for the case of homogeneity and heterogeneity in the estimation of the long-run variance, respectively. The Spectral Quadratic kernel was employed

***, ** and * imply rejection of the null hypothesis at 1, 5 and 10 %, respectively

worker, human capital, TFP and average annual hours worked (all expressed in logs of the value of the respective variable relative to its cross-country average).

We begin with the log of relative real physical capital per worker. As shown in the left part of Table 4.4, all panel unit root tests including those of Smith et al. (2004), Chang (2002), Breitung and Das (2005), Choi (2002), Moon and Perron (2004) and Pesaran (2007) fail to reject the unit root null hypothesis even at the 10 % level. Likewise, Panel A of Table 4.5 shows that the joint stationarity null hypothesis is rejected at the 1 % significance level with Hadri's (2000) statistic assuming cross-sectional independence and asymptotic normality, and at the 2.5 % level for the case of cross-sectional dependence, as reflected in the bootstrap critical values that are shifted to the right of the upper tail of the standard normal distribution (see Panel B of Table 4.5). Therefore, the evidence of a lack of stochastic convergence in real physical capital per worker appears overwhelming.

As regards the human capital index, the evidence reported in Table 4.6 appears clearly mixed. On the one hand, we are able to reject the unit root null hypothesis with three of the five bootstrap panel unit root tests of Smith et al. (2004) (Ψ_{LM}, Ψ_{Min} and Ψ_{WS}), the three combination panel unit root statistics of Choi (2002) and three of the four pooled panel unit root tests of Moon and Perron (2004). On the other, evidence pointing to a lack of stochastic convergence (also seen as divergence) is obtained from the $\Psi_{\bar{t}}$ and Ψ_{Max} statistics of Smith et al. (2004), the three nonlinear IV panel unit root tests of Chang (2002), the panel statistic of Breitung and Das (2005) and the four cross-sectionally augmented panel unit root tests of Pesaran (2007). The results from the application of Hadri's panel stationarity test (shown in Table 4.7) support the unit root hypothesis associated with a lack of stochastic convergence in human capital levels. This is because the joint stationarity null hypothesis is rejected at the 1 % level for the case of cross-independence and asymptotic normality, as well as at the 10 % level for the case of cross-sectional

Table 4.8 Panel unit root and stationarity tests: total factor productivity

	Trend specification: stochastic convergence		No trend specification: deterministic convergence	
	Statistic	*p*-value	Statistic	*p*-value
Smith et al. (2004)				
$\Psi_{\bar{t}}$	−2.282	0.166	−1.112	0.875
Ψ_{Max}	−1.826	0.166	−0.817	0.591
Ψ_{LM}	5.234	0.363	3.285	0.572
Ψ_{Min}	4.217	0.128	2.390	0.225
Ψ_{WS}	−2.187	0.240	−0.950	0.774
Chang (2002)				
S_{N1}	0.223	0.588	−0.131	0.448
S_{N2}	0.099	0.539	3.592	1.000
S_{N3}	1.316	0.906	1.360	0.913
Breitung and Das (2005)				
t_{rob}	0.840	0.800	0.482	0.685
Choi (2002)				
Modified inverse chi-square test (*Pm*)	2.926***	0.002	1.463*	0.072
Inverse normal test (*Z*)	−1.419*	0.078	−0.965	0.167
Modified logit test (L^*)	−1.434*	0.076	−1.057	0.145
Moon and Perron (2004)				
t_a^* (Quadratic spectral kernel)	−2.209**	0.014	−5.380***	0.000
t_b^* (Quadratic spectral kernel)	−2.459***	0.007	−3.587***	0.000
t_a^* (Bartlett kernel)	−2.229**	0.013	−5.355***	0.000
t_b^* (Bartlett kernel)	−2.507***	0.006	−3.617***	0.000
Pesaran (2007)				
CIPS	−2.274	0.585	−1.997	0.200
*CIPS**	−2.274	0.585	−1.997	0.200
Optimal lag truncation	3		2	
CP	41.397		51.633	
CZ	−0.172		−1.103	
Harris et al. (2005)				
$\hat{S}_k^F$			2.000**	0.023
No. factors (IC_1)			5	

Notes The bootstrap *p*-values for the five panel unit root tests of Smith et al. (2004) are computed employing 20,000 bootstrap replications and defining a block size equal to 30. The maximum lag order is set to 8. A general-to-specific procedure has been used to select the optimal lag-length. For the Moon and Perron (2004) and Harris et al. (2005) statistics we set the maximum number of factors to 5. The 1, 5 and 10 % critical values for the *CP* test (*CZ* test) are 78.49, 65.57 and 58.64 (−3.07, −2.23 and −1.75) for the specification without trends. The 1, 5 and 10 % critical values for the *CP* test (*CZ* test) are 78.90, 65.01 and 58.60 (−2.90, −2.05 and −1.59) for the specification with trends. These critical values are computed for T = 50 and N = 20. The $\hat{S}_k^F$ statistic is a panel stationarity test and the others are panel unit root tests

***, ** and * imply rejection of the null hypothesis at 1, 5 and 10 %, respectively

Table 4.9 Panel stationarity test of Hadri (2000): total factor productivity

	Trend specification: stochastic convergence				No trend specification: deterministic convergence			
Panel A: panel KPSS test assuming cross-sectional independence								
	Test		*p*-value		Test		*p*-value	
LM (Homogeneous)	6.388***		0.000		11.191***		0.000	
LM (Heterogeneous)	5.634***		0.000		8.82***		0.000	
Panel B: bootstrap critical values (assuming cross-section dependence)								
	10 %	5 %	2.5 %	1 %	10 %	5 %	2.5 %	1 %
LM (Homogeneous)	3.622	4.853	6.037	7.526	4.521	6.954	9.244	12.243
LM (Heterogeneous)	3.057	3.984	4.913	6.06	3.609	5.519	7.37	9.578

Notes The bootstrap critical values for Hadri's test are computed employing 20,000 bootstrap replications. LM (Homogeneous) and LM (Heterogeneous) denote the panel KPSS test of Hadri (2000) for the case of homogeneity and heterogeneity in the estimation of the long-run variance, respectively. The Spectral Quadratic kernel was employed

***, ** and * imply rejection of the null hypothesis at 1, 5 and 10 %, respectively

dependence and homogeneity in the long-run variance and at the 2.5 % level for the case of cross-dependence and heterogeneity in the estimation of the long-run variance. Hence, the overall evidence of stochastic convergence in human capital appears mixed.

As far as TFP is concerned, Table 4.8 provides evidence consistent with a unit root in the log of relative TFP levels in the case of the five modified bootstrap panel unit root tests of Smith et al. (2004), the three nonlinear IV panel unit root statistics of Chang (2002), the panel statistic of Breitung and Das (2005), and the four cross-sectionally augmented panel unit root tests of Pesaran (2007). However, the three combination panel unit root tests of Choi (2002) and the pooled panel unit root statistics of Moon and Perron (2004) reject the joint unit root null hypothesis at conventional significance levels. As regards Hadri's statistic, the evidence—shown in Table 4.9—favours the absence of stochastic convergence in TFP because the joint stationarity null hypothesis is strongly rejected both for the case of cross-independence (at the 1 % level) and for the case of cross-dependence (at the 2.5 % level). Hence, the picture that emerges for TFP is that of mixed evidence regarding stochastic convergence of TFP levels across OECD countries over the past four decades.

Finally, Table 4.10 contains the results from the application of the large battery of panel unit root tests to the log of relative average annual hours worked. Except for the Moon and Perron (2004) panel tests, the other panel unit root statistics fail to reject the joint non-stationarity null hypothesis. Likewise, Hadri's statistic (reported in Table 4.11) clearly supports the existence of a unit root in the log of relative average annual hours worked, as the joint stationarity null hypothesis is strongly rejected at the 1 % significance level, irrespective of the assumptions regarding cross-sectional correlation and heterogeneity in the computation of the residual

Table 4.10 Panel unit root and stationarity tests: annual average hours

	Trend specification: stochastic convergence		No trend specification: deterministic convergence	
	Statistic	p-value	Statistic	p-value
Smith et al. (2004)				
$\Psi_{\bar{t}}$	−1.631	0.945	−1.699	0.109
Ψ_{Max}	−1.333	0.855	−0.343	0.981
Ψ_{LM}	5.649	0.105	4.385	0.108
Ψ_{Min}	3.701	0.198	2.110	0.419
Ψ_{WS}	−1.782	0.932	−0.797	0.914
Chang (2002)				
S_{N1}	0.848	0.802	2.362	0.991
S_{N2}	−0.494	0.311	5.677	1.000
S_{N3}	1.022	0.847	3.966	1.000
Breitung and Das (2005)				
t_{rob}	0.333	0.631	0.911	0.819
Choi (2002)				
Modified inverse chi-square test (Pm)	−0.954	0.830	2.768***	0.003
Inverse normal test (Z)	0.788	0.785	−2.169**	0.015
Modified logit test (L)*	0.918	0.821	−2.258**	0.012
Moon and Perron (2004)				
t_a^* (Quadratic spectral kernel)	−1.803**	0.036	−6.932***	0.000
t_b^* (Quadratic spectral kernel)	−1.801**	0.036	−4.804***	0.000
t_a^* (Bartlett kernel)	−1.798**	0.036	−6.953***	0.000
t_b^* (Bartlett kernel)	−1.808**	0.035	−4.851***	0.000
Pesaran (2007)				
CIPS	−2.010	0.915	−1.768	0.500
*CIPS**	−2.010	0.915	−1.768	0.500
Optimal lag truncation	3		3	
CP	35.800		46.304	
CZ	1.458		−0.036	
Harris et al. (2005)				
$\hat{S}_k^F$			2.182**	0.015
No. factors (IC_1)			5	

Notes The bootstrap p-values for the five panel unit root tests of Smith et al. (2004) are computed employing 20,000 bootstrap replications and defining a block size equal to 30. The maximum lag order is set to 8. A general-to-specific procedure has been used to select the optimal lag-length. For the Moon and Perron (2004) and Harris et al. (2005) statistics we set the maximum number of factors to 5. The 1, 5 and 10 % critical values for the *CP* test (*CZ* test) are 78.49, 65.57 and 58.64 (−3.07, −2.23 and −1.75) for the specification without trends. The 1, 5 and 10 % critical values for the *CP* test (*CZ* test) are 78.90, 65.01 and 58.60 (−2.90, −2.05 and −1.59) for the specification with trends. These critical values are computed for T = 50 and N = 20. The $\hat{S}_k^F$ statistic is a panel stationarity test and the others are panel unit root tests

***, ** and * imply rejection of the null hypothesis at 1, 5 and 10 %, respectively

Table 4.11 Panel stationarity test of Hadri (2000): annual average hours

	Trend specification: stochastic convergence				No trend specification: deterministic convergence			
Panel A: panel KPSS test assuming cross-sectional independence								
	Test		*p*-value		Test		*p*-value	
LM (Homogeneous)	7.815***		0.000		12.135***		0.000	
LM (Heterogeneous)	7.202***		0.000		9.658***		0.000	
Panel B: bootstrap critical values (assuming cross-section dependence)								
	10 %	5 %	2.5 %	1 %	10 %	5 %	2.5 %	1 %
LM (Homogeneous)	3.465	4.699	5.873	7.549	4.459	6.854	9.295	12.109
LM (Heterogeneous)	2.980	3.943	4.863	6.241	3.541	5.489	7.316	9.572

Notes The bootstrap critical values for Hadri's test are computed employing 20,000 bootstrap replications. LM (Homogeneous) and LM (Heterogeneous) denote the panel KPSS test of Hadri (2000) for the case of homogeneity and heterogeneity in the estimation of the long-run variance, respectively. The Spectral Quadratic kernel was employed

***, ** and * imply rejection of the null hypothesis at 1, 5 and 10 %, respectively

long-run variance. Hence, the bulk of the evidence for average annual hours worked points to a lack of stochastic convergence.

Overall, with the exception of real physical capital per worker for which all panel statistics provide evidence of absence of stochastic convergence, for the other variables all panel tests fail to render support in the same direction because at least the Moon and Perron (2004) statistics reject the null hypothesis of a lack of stochastic convergence. In the case of human capital and TFP, other panel statistics like those of Choi (2002) also reject the joint unit root null hypothesis. Therefore, we can view the evidence of stochastic convergence as mixed for human capital and TFP, whereas the evidence lends support to a lack of stochastic convergence in real physical capital per worker and to a lower extent in real GDP per worker and average annual hours worked. These results appear to stand in stark contrast to the common expectation that real GDP per worker and hence its main sources (physical capital per worker, human capital and TFP) have all converged over the postwar era.

4.4 Analysis of Deterministic Convergence

Having studied the hypothesis of stochastic convergence, for the sake of completeness, we now shift the focus to investigate the stronger notion of deterministic convergence, which allows the value of the respective series in one country to move in parallel to the average value across countries over the postwar era. Of course, given that most of the evidence did not favour the existence of stochastic convergence across OECD countries, we do not expect to find widespread evidence supporting the existence of the stronger notion of deterministic convergence. This is indeed what the application of the whole battery of panel unit root and stationarity tests indicate.[3]

More specifically, the right part of Table 4.2 presents the results of the modified bootstrap panel unit root tests of Smith et al. (2004), the nonlinear IV panel statistics of Chang (2002), the Breitung and Das (2005) panel statistic, the combination panel unit root tests of Choi (2002), the pooled unit root tests of Moon and Perron (2004), the cross-sectionally augmented panel unit root tests of Pesaran (2007) and the factor-based panel stationarity test of Harris et al. (2005), and the right part of Table 4.3 reports the results from the application of the panel stationarity test of Hadri (2000). Remarkably, with the exception of the Ψ_{LM} and Ψ_{Min} panel unit root tests of Smith et al. (2004), the three combination panel tests of Choi (2002) and the pooled panel unit root statistics of Moon and Perron (2004), all the other panel procedures support the unit root hypothesis associated with a lack of deterministic convergence in real GDP per worker. Thus, there appears to be mixed evidence regarding the deterministic convergence hypothesis—though admittedly the majority of the panel statistics do not support the existence of deterministic convergence.

As with real GDP per worker, the unit root hypothesis for the no-trend specification associated with deterministic convergence in real physical capital per worker is not generally supported, except for the case of the Ψ_{LM} and Ψ_{Min} panel statistics, the three combination tests of Choi (2002) and the pooled statistics of Moon and Perron (2004)—see Tables 4.4 and 4.5. Hence, even though the evidence appears mixed, still most of the panel procedures support the absence of deterministic convergence in real physical capital per worker.

As regards the human capital index, the evidence regarding the presence of deterministic convergence in the series—shown in Tables 4.6 and 4.7—is clearly mixed. On the one hand, the more powerful bootstrap panel statistics of Smith et al. (2004), the nonlinear IV panel tests of Chang (2002), the panel test of Breitung and Das (2005), the cross-sectionally augmented combination panel statistics of Pesaran (2007) given by the inverse Chi-square test and the inverse normal test as well as the panel stationarity of Hadri (2000), all support the unit root hypothesis for the no-trend specification associated with the notion of deterministic convergence. On the other, the combination panel unit root tests of Choi (2002), the pooled panel statistics of Moon and Perron (2004), the cross-sectionally augmented IPS statistics of Pesaran (2007) and the panel stationarity test of Harris et al. (2005) favour the occurrence of deterministic convergence in human capital—since the joint stationarity null hypothesis is not rejected for the latter, whereas the joint nonstationarity null hypothesis is rejected for the others.

In the case of TFP, whose results from the application of the panel unit root and stationarity tests appear in Tables 4.8 and 4.9, the evidence mostly favours the unit

[3] To the set of panel statistics employed in the analysis of stochastic convergence, we add the panel stationarity test of Harris et al. (2005), which was developed only for the no-trend case.

root hypothesis consistent with the absence of deterministic convergence among OECD countries because, of all procedures, only the Moon and Perron (2004) statistics and the modified inverse Chi-square test of Choi (2002) are able to reject that hypothesis. Finally, Tables 4.10 and 4.11 report the results for the average annual hours worked. The evidence supportive of deterministic convergence appears somewhat mixed, though admittedly most of the results reject the hypothesis of deterministic convergence. Indeed, the panel unit root tests of Smith et al. (2004), Chang (2002), Breitung and Das (2005) and Pesaran (2007) fail to reject the joint non-stationarity null hypothesis, and the panel stationarity tests of Hadri (2000) and Harris et al. (2005) strongly reject the joint stationarity null hypothesis, thus providing confirmatory evidence of the lack of deterministic convergence. Only with the panel unit root statistics of Choi (2002) and Moon and Perron (2004) are we able to reject the joint non-stationarity null hypothesis.

Summing up, there is no clear-cut evidence of deterministic convergence in any of the five series investigated: in neither real GDP per worker nor its sources given by real physical capital per worker, human capital, TFP and average annual hours worked. Rather the opposite, the evidence appears to support a lack of deterministic convergence, particularly for TFP and to a lower extent for real GDP per worker, real physical capital per worker and average annual hours worked. The evidence appears clearly mixed for the human capital index, as given by a more balanced account of the panel procedures that support one or the other hypothesis.

In the next chapter, we apply a less restrictive framework to the one employed in this chapter in an attempt to shed some further light on the presence or absence of the stochastic and deterministic notions of convergence. Hopefully, the use of the recently developed Panel Analysis of Non-stationarity in Idiosyncratic and Common components (PANIC) procedure by Bai and Ng (2004a) will enable us to provide more clear-cut evidence in support of or against the two notions of convergence, rather than providing mixed results as has been mostly the case in the analysis implemented so far.

Chapter 5
PANIC Approach

Abstract This chapter presents the main advantages of the PANIC approach versus other panel unit root and stationarity tests. First, PANIC enables us to allow for strong forms of cross-sectional dependence in the data such as cross-cointegration. Second, it allows us to decompose the observed series into a common and an idiosyncratic component, as well as to determine the source of nonstationarity in the observed series, that is, whether it stems from the common factor(s) and/or the idiosyncratic components. Third, unlike other factor-based panel unit root tests, PANIC is flexible enough as to allow for a different order of integration in both components. Fourth, PANIC acts as a cointegration framework that can be applied to the log of the respective series, thereby enabling us to relax the homogeneity assumption previously imposed when focusing on relative series.

Keywords Time series convergence · PANIC · Cointegration

5.1 Methodological and Conceptual Limitations of the Previous Analysis

Unlike several second-generation panel unit root tests used above such as the non-linear IV panel unit root tests of Chang (2002), the bootstrap panel unit root tests of Smith et al. (2004), the Breitung and Das (2005) test and the bootstrap version of the panel stationarity test of Hadri (2000) that only allow for weak forms of cross-sectional dependence such as contemporaneous short-run cross-correlation, some panel unit root tests based on linear factor models are able to allow for stronger forms of cross-dependence such as cross-sectional cointegration.[1] Among the panel procedures employing a factor structure, we find Moon and Perron (2004), Pesaran (2007) and Bai and Ng (2004a, b). Whereas Pesaran (2007) only allows for one common factor, Moon and Perron (2004) and Bai and Ng (2004a, b) allow for

[1] See Breitung and Pesaran (2008) for an overview of the methods.

M. Hernández Salmerón and D. Romero-Ávila, *Convergence in Output and Its Sources Among Industrialised Countries*, SpringerBriefs in Economics, DOI 10.1007/978-3-319-13635-6_5

multiple common factors. However, only the panel tests of Bai and Ng (2004a, b) are general enough to allow for cointegration across units, which implies that the observed series can contain common stochastic trends.[2] In fact, under this framework the observed series is decomposed into a common component and an idiosyncratic component, and if the latter component is found to be I(0) and the former is found to be I(1), the observed series and the nonstationary common factor would be cointegrated. In that particular case of cross-cointegration, the tests of Pesaran (2007) and Moon and Perron (2004) are likely to exhibit size distortions, as the common trends may be confused with the common factors and thus removed from the data in the defactoring process. Therefore, the tests on the observed series appear to yield stationarity if the remaining idiosyncratic component is stationary, despite the fact there are non-stationary common factors.[3]

In the previous analysis, the Moon and Perron (2004) statistics were generally able to reject the unit root null hypothesis, which may have been caused by the size distortions exhibited by the panel tests in the presence of common stochastic trends driving the observed series. Therefore, in the next chapter that presents the results from the application of the PANIC procedures to the series under study, we will be able to determine the presence or absence of common stochastic trends in the series, which may have been responsible for the widespread rejection of the unit root hull hypothesis with the Moon and Perron (2004) statistics. In contrast, Bai and Ng (2004a, b)'s PANIC framework does not suffer from such size distortions by not only allowing for non-stationary idiosyncratic components but also for common stochastic components.

In short, the use of the PANIC methodology conveys several important advantages over the analysis conducted above and over previous studies in the field of time-series convergence using panel methods. First, it enables us to allow for strong forms of cross-sectional dependence in the data such as cross-cointegration. This is essential since failure to allow for cross-sectional correlation, when it is present in the data, leads to severe size distortions (see O'Connell 1998; Maddala and Wu 1999; Banerjee et al. 2005). Second, the PANIC approach allows us to decompose the observed real GDP per worker, real physical capital per worker, human capital, TFP and average annual hours worked into a common and an idiosyncratic component, and as a byproduct, to determine the source of nonstationarity in the observed series, that is, whether it stems from the common factor(s) and/or the idiosyncratic components. Third, unlike other panel unit root tests allowing for a factor structure in the data such as those of Moon and Perron (2004) and Pesaran (2007) that assume the same order of integration for both the common

[2] See Gengenbach et al. (2010, pp. 126–129) for a detailed description of the differences and similarities among the Moon and Perron (2004), Pesaran (2007) and Bai and Ng (2004a) panel unit root tests.

[3] Gengenbach et al. (2010, p. 134) provide simulation evidence that lends support to the large size distortions associated with the panel unit root tests of Moon and Perron (2004) and Pesaran (2007) in the event of non-stationary common factors and a near-unit root in the idiosyncratic component, which is the case of cross-sectional cointegration.

and idiosyncratic components, the PANIC framework is flexible enough as to allow for a different order of integration in both components.

Regarding the conceptual limitation of the previous analysis, we have that by applying the panel unit root and stationarity statistics to the log of the relative series —which is equivalent to the log of the series minus the log of the average of the series across panel members—one is implicitly assuming a common slope of unity in the relationship between the log of a series and the log of the average (i.e., $\log y_{it} - \beta_i \log \bar{y}_t$ with $\beta_i = 1$ for all i). Therefore, the hypothesis of stationarity in the log of the relative series, consistent with the existence of time series convergence, requires the series $\log y_{it}$ and $\log \bar{y}_t$ to be cointegrated with a cointegrating vector [1,−1]. This implies that homogeneity is imposed for all i, without being previously tested before the panel unit root and stationarity tests were applied to the relative series.

An alternative and less restrictive approach consists of testing for a single common stochastic trend among a set of I(1) series (in our case the 21 countries' series for each of the respective variable analysed) driving the observed series over time. Pairwise convergence would be confirmed through the existence of $N - 1$ cointegrating vectors among the N countries investigated. One possible approach to this is to use the common trend framework of Stock and Watson (1988) or the Johansen (1988)'s maximum likelihood approach, which requires the estimation of a fully specified vector autoregression system—with the data requirements that involves for this framework to perform well. In addition, one could have applied the panel unit root and stationarity tests to the log of the relative series computed with respect to a base country instead of the cross-section average. In that case, the results would be sensitive to the choice of base country.

By relaxing the homogeneity assumption, we can apply the PANIC framework to the log of real GDP per worker and its sources rather than to the relative series, so that we can determine the presence of a common stochastic trend driving the observed series for each respective variable. If that was the case, there would be evidence of either pairwise stochastic or deterministic convergence, depending on whether the PANIC specification includes deterministic linear trends or not. Most importantly for the analysis of time series convergence, PANIC can be used as a cointegration analysis among the individual series forming each of the five panels for real GDP per worker, real physical capital per worker, human capital, TFP and average annual hours worked, respectively. The system of the N series forming each panel can be decomposed into a nonstationary part explained by the common stochastic trends ($\hat{r}_1$) in addition to $N - \hat{r}_1$ cointegrating vectors involving stationary linear combinations of the individual series forming the panel. In short, if we find evidence of a common stochastic trend driving the observed series, combined with the existence of jointly stationary idiosyncratic series, this would indicate the presence of pairwise cointegration among the individual series involved, which would be driven by a nonstationary common factor linking all individual series (involving real GDP per worker or each of the four output sources variables) over time. This would show up as convergence patterns exhibited by the individual series over time. If the evidence, instead, indicates the existence of two common stochastic trends (rather than one), there would be $N-2$ cointegrating vectors, which would imply weaker evidence of time-series convergence relative to the case of pairwise convergence. In the extreme case in which there are no co-integrating vectors, there would be N independent common stochastic trends, and zero evidence of cross-cointegration and convergence. At the other end, if there are no common stochastic trends ($\hat{r}_1 = 0$), it means that there are N cointegrating vectors, implying linear combinations of the individual series forming each panel. This would indicate that all common factors are I(0) and the individual series are stationary (Gengenbach et al. 2010, p. 128).

5.2 PANIC Methodology

We first model the observed data on the variable considered (denoted by Y_{it}) expressed in log terms as the sum of a deterministic part, a common component and an idiosyncratic error term:

$$Y_{it} = D_{it} + \lambda_i' F_t + e_{it} \tag{5.1}$$

where λ_i is an $r \times 1$ vector of factor loadings, F_t is an $r \times 1$ vector of common factors, and e_{it} is the idiosyncratic component. D_{it} can contain a constant and a linear trend, depending on the notion of time-series convergence studied. Given that λ_i and F_t can only be estimated consistently when $e_{it} \sim I(0)$, we estimate a model in first-differences like $\Delta Y_{it} = \lambda_i' f_t + z_{it}$, where $z_{it} = \Delta e_{it}$ and $f_t = \Delta F_t$.[4] We next use principal components to estimate the common factors $\hat{f}_t$, the corresponding factor loadings $\hat{\lambda}_i$ and the residuals $\hat{z}_{it} = \Delta Y_{it} - \hat{\lambda}_i' \hat{f}_t$, which enables us to preserve the order of integration of F_t and e_{it}. In the PANIC framework the common factors and idiosyncratic components are estimated consistently irrespective of their order of integration. As in Bai and Ng (2002), Y_{it} is normalised for each cross-section unit to have a unit variance. The common factors and the residuals are then recumulated as follows: $\hat{F}_t = \sum_{s=2}^{t} \hat{f}_s$ and $\hat{e}_{it} = \sum_{s=2}^{t} \hat{z}_{is}$, which can be used to test for a unit root in the common and idiosyncratic components, respectively.

Prior to testing for a unit root in the common and idiosyncratic components, we employ information criteria to establish the number of common factors present in the panels of real GDP per worker, real physical capital per worker, human capital,

[4] This representation corresponds to the factor model with a constant. For the representation in the case of a specification with a trend for the analysis of stochastic convergence, we have $Y_{it} = c_i + \beta_i t + \lambda_i' F_t + e_{it}$, where $\Delta Y_{it} = \beta_i + \lambda_i' \Delta F_t + \Delta e_{it}$. Letting $\overline{\Delta F} = (T-1)^{-1} \sum_{t=2}^{T} \Delta F_t$, $\overline{\Delta e_i} = (T-1)^{-1} \sum_{t=2}^{T} \Delta e_{it}$, and $\overline{\Delta Y_i} = (T-1)^{-1} \sum_{t=2}^{T} \Delta Y_{it}$, we proceed as follows: $\Delta Y_{it} - \overline{\Delta Y_i} = \lambda_i' (\Delta F_t - \overline{\Delta F}) + (\Delta e_{it} - \overline{\Delta e_i})$. This can be rewritten as $y_{it} = \lambda_i' f_t + z_{it}$, where $y_{it} = \Delta Y_{it} - \overline{\Delta Y_i}$, $f_t = \Delta F_t - \overline{\Delta F}$ and $z_{it} = \Delta e_{it} - \overline{\Delta e_i}$.

TFP and average annual hours worked. We do so with the BIC_3 information criterion:

$$BIC_3(k) = \hat{\sigma}_e^2(k) + k\hat{\sigma}_e^2(k_{\max})\left(\frac{(N+T-k)\ln(NT)}{NT}\right) \tag{5.2}$$

where k is the number of factors included in the model, $\hat{\sigma}_e^2(k)$ is the variance of the estimated idiosyncratic components, and $\hat{\sigma}_e^2(k_{\max})$ is the variance of the idiosyncratic components estimated with the maximum number of factors ($k_{\max} = 5$).[5] The optimal number of common factors $\hat{k}$ is selected by applying arg $\min_{0 \le k \le 5} BIC_3(k)$. We employ the BIC_3 procedure instead of other alternatives (like the IC_p information criteria) because for a sufficiently general framework in which the idiosyncratic errors can be serially correlated and cross-correlated, the BIC_3 criterion exhibits very good properties, as shown in Tables 7 and 8 in Bai and Ng (2002). Likewise, Moon and Perron (2007, p. 387) note that the BIC_3 criterion "performs better in selecting the number of factors when min(N, T) is small (≤20)". For the sake of robustness, we also present the IC_1, IC_2 and IC_3 panel information criteria of Bai and Ng (2002), which—unlike their PC_p counterparts—do not depend on the maximum number of factors. The expression for the three IC_p criteria is $\ln(\hat{\sigma}_e^2(k)) + kg(N,T)$, where $g(N, T)$ is the penalty function that depends on both T and N. More specifically, $g(N, T)$ equals $\left(\frac{N+T}{NT}\right)\ln\left(\frac{NT}{N+T}\right)$, $\left(\frac{N+T}{NT}\right)\ln\left(C_{NT}^2\right)$ and $\frac{\ln C_{NT}^2}{C_{NT}^2}$ for IC_1, IC_2 and IC_3, respectively, where $C_{NT}^2 = \min(N,T)$.[6]

5.2.1 Analysis of the Idiosyncratic Component

As regards the analysis of the idiosyncratic component, Bai and Ng (2004a) estimate standard ADF specifications for a unit root in the idiosyncratic series:

$$\Delta\hat{e}_{it} = \delta_{i,0}\hat{e}_{i,t-1} + \sum_{j=1}^{p_i}\delta_{i,j}\Delta\hat{e}_{i,t-j} + u_{it} \tag{5.3}$$

The ADF t-statistic for testing $\delta_{i,0} = 0$ is denoted by $ADF_{\hat{e}}^c(i)$ or $ADF_{\hat{e}}^\tau(i)$ for the cases of only a constant and a constant and a linear trend in specification (5.3),

5 The second argument in the loss function represents the penalty for overfitting, which tries to correct for the fact that models with a larger number of factors can at least fit as good as models with fewer common factors, but efficiency is reduced with the estimation of more factor loading parameters (Bai and Ng 2002).

6 The BIC_3 procedure developed in Bai and Ng (2002) clearly outperforms alternative information criteria, especially for short-N panels, which fits our panel dataset (see Bai and Ng 2002, pp. 205–207; Moon and Perron 2007, p. 387; Gengenbach et al. 2010, p. 134).

respectively.[7] In order to increase statistical power, Bai and Ng (2004a) employ pooled statistics based on the Fisher-type inverse chi-square tests of Maddala and Wu (1999) and Choi (2001), which can only be used when the idiosyncratic components are cross-sectionally independent.[8] Letting $\pi^c_{\hat{e}}(i)$ be the p-value associated with $ADF^c_{\hat{e}}(i)$, the pooled statistics are constructed as follows:[9]

$$P^c_{\hat{e}} = -2\sum_{i=1}^{N} \log \pi^c_{\hat{e}}(i) \xrightarrow{d} \chi^2_{(2N)} \quad \text{for } N \text{ fixed}, \ T \to \infty, \tag{5.4}$$

$$Z^c_{\hat{e}} = \frac{-\sum_{i=1}^{N} \log \pi^c_{\hat{e}}(i) - N}{\sqrt{N}} \xrightarrow{d} N(0,1) \quad \text{for } N, \ T \to \infty. \tag{5.5}$$

5.2.2 Analysis of the Common Component

As far as the analysis of the common component is concerned, we proceed differently depending on whether the panel information criterion BIC_3 of Bai and Ng (2002) identifies only one common factor or more than one. In testing for non-stationarity in the common component, we employ a standard ADF statistic for the case of a single common factor ($k = 1$) or a rank test when $k > 1$. When the whole panel only contains a single common factor, we estimate an ADF specification for $\hat{F}_t$ with the same deterministic components as in model (5.1):

$$\Delta\hat{F}_t = D_t + \gamma_0\hat{F}_{t-1} + \sum_{j=1}^{p} \gamma_j \Delta\hat{F}_{t-j} + v_{it} \tag{5.6}$$

The corresponding ADF t-statistics are denoted by $ADF^c_{\hat{F}}$ and $ADF^\tau_{\hat{F}}$ and are characterised by the limiting distribution of the Dickey and Fuller (1979) test for the specifications with only a constant, and a constant and a trend, respectively. For the case of multiple common factors, the number of common stochastic trends ($\hat{r}_1$) present in the common factors is determined using the modified rank tests labelled as

[7] The asymptotic distribution of $ADF^c_{\hat{e}}(i)$ is the same as the Dickey-Fuller distribution for the case of no constant, while the asymptotic distribution of the $ADF^\tau_{\hat{e}}(i)$ statistic is proportional to the reciprocal of a Brownian bridge.

[8] If the observed series are correctly decomposed into the common and idiosyncratic components, the latter should be cross-sectionally independent.

[9] The same holds for the case of a trend, where $\pi^\tau_{\hat{e}}(i)$ is the p-value associated with $ADF^\tau_{\hat{e}}(i)$. The pooled statistics for the trend specification for the analysis of stochastic convergence are denoted as $P^\tau_{\hat{e}}$ and $Z^\tau_{\hat{e}}$. Note that we do not pool individual unit root tests for the observed series, since under a factor structure the limiting distribution of the test would contain terms that are common across units. In contrast, "pooling of tests for $\hat{e}_{it}$ is asymptotically valid under the more plausible assumption that $\hat{e}_{it}$ is independent across i" (Bai and Ng 2004a, p. 1140).

the filter test MQ_f that assumes that the non-stationary components are represented by finite order vector autoregressive processes and the corrected test MQ_c that allows the unit root processes to exhibit more general dynamics. In order to determine the number of stochastic trends in the system, we follow a sequential testing procedure, in which we first assume that the number of stochastic trends is equal to the number of common factors ($m = k$). Thus, we specify the null hypothesis that there are m stochastic trends against the alternative hypothesis of less than m common stochastic trends. If the null hypothesis is rejected, we then specify the null hypothesis of $m - 1$ stochastic trends, continuing this process until the null hypothesis is not rejected or when $m = 0$ is achieved, in which case there are no common stochastic trends. The critical values of the MQ_f and MQ_c rank statistics are provided in Table 1 in Bai and Ng (2004a).[10] Since the rank tests normally lack power to reject the null hypothesis, and as a result they support the existence of a number of common stochastic trends equal to the number of common factors, we apply the BIC_3 information criteria of Bai (2004) to determining the number of *non-stationary* common factors within the set of common factors previously identified. Unlike the information criteria to determine the optimal number of common factors (stationary and non-stationary) in Bai and Ng (2004a, b) that was applied to first-differenced data, the BIC_3 panel information criteria to determine the number of *non-stationary* common factors proposed by Bai (2004) is applied to level data. In addition, the consistency of Bai (2004)'s information criteria requires the idiosyncratic component to be I(0), which we will find below to be the case.

[10] For a panel cointegration rank testing procedure with cross-section dependence, see Carrion-i-Silvestre and Surdeanu (2011).

Chapter 6
PANIC Results

Abstract The analysis of stochastic convergence via PANIC provides strong evidence of convergence patterns in the series of log TFP, as given by the existence of pairwise cointegration among individual series, as well as weaker evidence of convergence in real GDP per worker and average annual hours worked (which exhibited two common stochastic trends) and yet weaker evidence of convergence in real physical capital per worker and human capital (which exhibited three common stochastic trends). As for the analysis of deterministic convergence, there is some evidence of convergence in real GDP per worker and average annual hours worked, and to a lower extent in real physical capital per worker and human capital, but the evidence for log TFP points to a lack of deterministic convergence.

Keywords Stochastic convergence · Deterministic convergence · PANIC · Factor models

After having presented the econometric methodology behind the PANIC approach, we now proceed to present the results from its application. There are two main reasons for applying this framework. First, the panel unit root and stationarity tests used in Chap. 4 either only allow for weak forms of cross-sectional dependence or preclude the possibility of having cross-cointegration among members of the panel. Second, the PANIC approach allows us to determine the source of nonstationarity, that is, whether it is present in the idiosyncratic components and/or in the common factors. Third and most important for our analysis, the PANIC framework can be used as a cointegration testing procedure that can be applied to the log of the series, and hence does not require transforming the series into relative values with respect to their average.

6.1 Determining the Optimal Number of Common Factors

Before testing for a unit root in the idiosyncratic series and common factors in which the individual series forming each of the five panels are decomposed, we estimate the common factors through principal components and then select the

M. Hernández Salmerón and D. Romero-Ávila, *Convergence in Output and Its Sources Among Industrialised Countries*,
SpringerBriefs in Economics, DOI 10.1007/978-3-319-13635-6_6

number of factors present in the five panels investigated corresponding to log real GDP per worker, log real physical capital per worker, log human capital, log TFP and log average annual hours worked. Even though there are several information criteria to determine the optimal number of common factors in each panel, we base our conclusions on the BIC_3 procedure developed in Bai and Ng (2002), which outperforms alternative information criteria for short-N panels (see Bai and Ng 2002, pp. 205–207; Moon and Perron 2007, p. 387; Gengenbach et al. 2010, p. 134). Tables 6.1, 6.2, 6.3, 6.4 and 6.5 report the results from the application of the IC_1, IC_2, IC_3 and BIC_3 information criteria to the five panels containing the respective variable for the sample of 21 OECD countries over the period

Table 6.1 Information criteria. Real GDP per worker

Number of factors (k)	$IC_1(k)$	$IC_2(k)$	$IC_3(k)$	$BIC_3(k)$
0	−7.851	−7.851	−7.851	0.000389
1	−8.154	−8.124	−8.198	0.000282
2	−8.231	−8.171	−8.319	0.000270*
3	−8.238	−8.148	−8.371	0.000278
4	−8.288	−8.169	−8.466	0.000286
5	−8.341*	−8.192*	−8.564*	0.000299

Notes * represents the lowest value of the information criteria. See the text for the equations associated with the information criteria

Table 6.2 Information criteria. Real physical capital per worker

Number of factors (k)	$IC_1(k)$	$IC_2(k)$	$IC_3(k)$	$BIC_3(k)$
0	−7.950	−7.950	−7.950	0.000353
1	−8.375	−8.346	−8.420	0.000222
2	−8.527	−8.468	−8.616	0.000196
3	−8.588	−8.499	−8.722	0.000195*
4	−8.654	−8.535	−8.832	0.000199
5	−8.701*	−8.552*	−8.923*	0.000209

Notes * represents the lowest value of the information criteria. See the text for the equations associated with the information criteria

Table 6.3 Information criteria. Human capital index

Number of factors (k)	$IC_1(k)$	$IC_2(k)$	$IC_3(k)$	$BIC_3(k)$
0	−10.567	−10.567	−10.567	0.0000257
1	−10.881	−10.851	−10.926	0.0000163
2	−11.125	−11.066	−11.214	0.0000116
3	−11.443	−11.354	−11.577	0.0000083
4	−11.851	−11.731	−12.028	0.0000063
5	−12.396*	−12.247*	−12.618*	0.0000052*

Notes * represents the lowest value of the information criteria. See the text for the equations associated with the information criteria

Table 6.4 Information criteria. Total factor productivity

Number of factors (k)	$IC_1(k)$	$IC_2(k)$	$IC_3(k)$	$BIC_3(k)$
0	−7.988	−7.988	−7.988	0.000339
1	−8.278	−8.248	−8.322	0.000252
2	−8.327	−8.268	−8.416	0.000247*
3	−8.357	−8.267	−8.490	0.000254
4	−8.383	−8.263	−8.560	0.000265
5	−8.404*	−8.255*	−8.627*	0.000281

Notes * represents the lowest value of the information criteria. See the text for the equations associated with the information criteria

Table 6.5 Information criteria. Annual average hours

Number of factors (k)	$IC_1(k)$	$IC_2(k)$	$IC_3(k)$	$BIC_3(k)$
0	−9.2809	−9.2809	−9.2809	0.0000932
1	−9.318	−9.2876	−9.3625	0.0000884
2	−9.3541	−9.2933	−9.4431	0.0000871*
3	−9.4121	−9.3209	−9.5456	0.0000874
4	−9.4242	−9.3026	−9.6021	0.0000919
5	−9.468*	−9.316*	−9.690*	0.0000965

Notes * represents the lowest value of the information criteria. See the text for the equations associated with the information criteria

1970–2011. For a maximum number of common factors equal to five, the BIC_3 procedure selects two common factors in log real GDP per worker, three common factors in log real physical capital per worker, five common factors in log human capital, and two common factors in both log TFP and log average annual hours worked. In the case of the IC_p criteria, they always select the maximum number of common factors (5) for the five panels. For the reasons provided above, we draw on the results obtained with the BIC_3 criterion which, with the exception of the human capital index, selects an optimal number of common factors lower than the maximum allowed.

6.2 Applying the PANIC Approach to Log Real GDP per Worker and Its Sources

Tables 6.6, 6.7, 6.8, 6.9 and 6.10 present the results from the application of the PANIC procedures to real GDP per worker, real physical capital per worker, human capital, TFP and average annual hours worked, respectively. Panel A in each table presents the pooled Fisher-type inverse Chi-square statistics of Maddala and Wu (1999) and Choi (2001), and Panel B presents the information regarding the number of common factors and the number of common stochastic trends contained in the

Table 6.6 PANIC analysis of log real GDP per worker

	Trend specification: stochastic convergence		No trend specification: deterministic convergence	
	Statistic	*p*-value	Statistic	*p*-value
Panel A: idiosyncratic component				
Bai and Ng (2004) pooled statistics				
$P_{\hat{e}}$	4.588***	0.000	2.177**	0.015
$Z_{\hat{e}}$	84.052***	0.000	61.951**	0.024
Panel B: number of common factors (k) & common stochastic trends ($\hat{r}_1$)				
No. factors (BIC_3)	2		2	
MQ_c	2		2	
MQ_f	2		2	
BIC_3 *(level)*	2		2	

	Rank test	Critical values			Rank test	Critical values		
	MQ_c^{τ}	1 %	5 %	10 %	MQ_c^{c}	1 %	5 %	10 %
$\hat{r}_1 = 2$	−6.015	−38.619	−31.356	−27.435	−1.408	−31.621	−23.535	−19.923
$\hat{r}_1 = 1$	−10.991	−29.246	−21.313	−17.829	−12.991	−20.151	−13.730	−11.022
	MQ_f^{τ}	1 %	5 %	10 %	MQ_f^{c}	1 %	5 %	10 %
$\hat{r}_1 = 2$	−2.348	−38.619	−31.356	−27.435	−0.371	−31.621	−23.535	−19.923
$\hat{r}_1 = 1$	−2.792	−29.246	−21.313	−17.829	−2.436	−20.151	−13.730	−11.022

Notes The augmented autoregressions employed in the ADF analysis select the optimal lag-order with the *t-sig* criterion of Ng and Perron (1995), setting a maximum lag-order equal to 8. The information criterion BIC_3 is employed to choose the optimal rank. $P_{\hat{e}}$ is distributed as χ^2_{42}, with 1, 5 and 10 % critical values equal to 66.206, 58.124 and 54.090, respectively. $Z_{\hat{e}}$ is distributed as N(0,1) with 1, 5 and 10 % critical values of 2.326, 1.645 and 1.282
***, ** and * imply rejection of the null hypothesis at 1, 5 and 10 %, respectively
Since $k > 1$, the estimated number of $\hat{r}_1$ stochastic trends in the common factors must be determined. We employ the filtered test MQ_f, the corrected test MQ_c and the BIC_3 criterion applied to level data in order to estimate $\hat{r}_1$

Table 6.7 PANIC analysis of log real physical capital per worker

	Trend specification: stochastic convergence		No trend specification: deterministic convergence	
	Statistic	*p*-value	Statistic	*p*-value
Panel A: idiosyncratic component				
Bai and Ng (2004) pooled statistics				
$P_{\hat{e}}$	8.727***	0.000	4.244***	0.000
$Z_{\hat{e}}$	121.981***	0.000	80.901***	0.000
Panel B: number of common factors (k) & common stochastic trends ($\hat{r}_1$)				
No. factors (BIC_3)	3		3	
MQ_c	3		3	
MQ_f	3		3	
BIC_3 *(level)*	3		3	

	Rank test	Critical values			Rank test	Critical values		
	MQ_c^{τ}	1 %	5 %	10 %	MQ_c^{c}	1 %	5 %	10 %
$\hat{r}_1 = 3$	−2.107	−50.019	−40.180	−35.685	−1.429	−41.064	−32.296	−28.399
$\hat{r}_1 = 2$	−1.844	−38.619	−31.356	−27.435	−3.739	−31.621	−23.535	−19.923
$\hat{r}_1 = 1$	−11.988	−29.246	−21.313	−17.829	−10.570	−20.151	−13.730	−11.022
	MQ_f^{τ}	1 %	5 %	10 %	MQ_f^{c}	1 %	5 %	10 %
$\hat{r}_1 = 3$	−0.550	−50.019	−40.180	−35.685	−0.330	−41.064	−32.296	−28.399
$\hat{r}_1 = 2$	−4.008	−38.619	−31.356	−27.435	−2.071	−31.621	−23.535	−19.923
$\hat{r}_1 = 1$	−11.876	−29.246	−21.313	−17.829	−5.722	−20.151	−13.730	−11.022

Notes The augmented autoregressions employed in the ADF analysis select the optimal lag-order with the *t-sig* criterion of Ng and Perron (1995), setting a maximum lag-order equal to 8. The information criterion BIC_3 is employed to choose the optimal rank. $P_{\hat{e}}$ is distributed as χ^2_{42}, with 1, 5 and 10 % critical values equal to 66.206, 58.124 and 54.090, respectively. $Z_{\hat{e}}$ is distributed as N(0,1) with 1, 5 and 10 % critical values of 2.326, 1.645 and 1.282

***, ** and * imply rejection of the null hypothesis at 1, 5 and 10 %, respectively

Since $k > 1$, the estimated number of $\hat{r}_1$ stochastic trends in the common factors must be determined. We employ the filtered test MQ_f, the corrected test MQ_c and the BIC_3 criterion applied to level data in order to estimate $\hat{r}_1$

Table 6.8 PANIC analysis of log human capital index

	Trend specification: stochastic convergence		No trend specification: deterministic convergence	
	Statistic	*p*-value	Statistic	*p*-value
Panel A: idiosyncratic component				
Bai and Ng (2004) pooled statistics				
$P_{\hat{e}}$	5.698***	0.000	4.479***	0.000
$Z_{\hat{e}}$	94.219***	0.000	83.049***	0.000
Panel B: number of common factors (k) & common stochastic trends ($\hat{r}_1$)				
No. factors (BIC_3)	5		5	
MQ_c	5		5	
MQ_f	5		5	
BIC_3 *(level)*	3		3	

	Rank test	Critical values			Rank test	Critical values		
	MQ_c^{τ}	1 %	5 %	10 %	MQ_c^{c}	1 %	5 %	10 %
$\hat{r}_1 = 5$	−2.367	−64.729	−55.808	−55.286	−0.725	−58.383	−48.617	−44.111
$\hat{r}_1 = 4$	−1.794	−58.140	−48.421	−44.079	−7.894	−48.501	−40.442	−36.592
$\hat{r}_1 = 3$	−8.287	−50.019	−40.180	−35.685	−8.163	−41.064	−32.296	−28.399
$\hat{r}_1 = 2$	−14.225	−38.619	−31.356	−27.435	−10.695	−31.621	−23.535	−19.923
$\hat{r}_1 = 1$	−13.110	−29.246	−21.313	−17.829	−12.876	−20.151	−13.730	−11.022
	MQ_f^{τ}	1 %	5 %	10 %	MQ_f^{c}	1 %	5 %	10 %
$\hat{r}_1 = 5$	−3.430	−64.729	−55.808	−55.286	−1.586	−58.383	−48.617	−44.111
$\hat{r}_1 = 4$	−5.329	−58.140	−48.421	−44.079	−1.784	−48.501	−40.442	−36.592
$\hat{r}_1 = 3$	−11.101	−50.019	−40.180	−35.685	−6.212	−41.064	−32.296	−28.399
$\hat{r}_1 = 2$	−14.456	−38.619	−31.356	−27.435	−14.512	−31.621	−23.535	−19.923
$\hat{r}_1 = 1$	−17.560	−29.246	−21.313	−17.829	−16.927	−20.151	−13.730	−11.022

Notes The augmented autoregressions employed in the ADF analysis select the optimal lag-order with the *t-sig* criterion of Ng and Perron (1995), setting a maximum lag-order equal to 8. The information criterion BIC_3 is employed to choose the optimal rank. $P_{\hat{e}}$ is distributed as χ^2_{42}, with 1, 5 and 10 % critical values equal to 66.206, 58.124 and 54.090, respectively. $Z_{\hat{e}}$ is distributed as N(0,1) with 1, 5 and 10 % critical values of 2.326, 1.645 and 1.282

***, ** and * imply rejection of the null hypothesis at 1, 5 and 10 %, respectively

Since $k > 1$, the estimated number of $\hat{r}_1$ stochastic trends in the common factors must be determined. We employ the filtered test MQ_f, the corrected test MQ_c and the BIC_3 criterion applied to level data in order to estimate $\hat{r}_1$

Table 6.9 PANIC analysis of log total factor productivity

	Trend specification: stochastic convergence		No trend specification: deterministic convergence	
	Statistic	*p*-value	Statistic	*p*-value
Panel A: idiosyncratic component				
Bai and Ng (2004) pooled statistics				
$P_{\hat{e}}$	7.277***	0.000	0.515	0.303
$Z_{\hat{e}}$	108.697***	0.000	46.718	0.285
Panel B: number of common factors (k) & common stochastic trends ($\hat{r}_1$)				
No. factors (BIC_3)	2		2	
MQ_c	2		2	
MQ_f	2		2	
BIC_3 (*level*)	1		1	

	Rank test	Critical values			Rank test	Critical values		
	MQ_c^{τ}	1 %	5 %	10 %	MQ_c^{c}	1 %	5 %	10 %
$\hat{r}_1 = 2$	−5.919	−38.619	−31.356	−27.435	−1.611	−31.621	−23.535	−19.923
$\hat{r}_1 = 1$	−10.570	−29.246	−21.313	−17.829	−11.323	−20.151	−13.730	−11.022
	MQ_f^{τ}	1 %	5 %	10 %	MQ_f^{c}	1 %	5 %	10 %
$\hat{r}_1 = 2$	−5.958	−38.619	−31.356	−27.435	−1.535	−31.621	−23.535	−19.923
$\hat{r}_1 = 1$	−9.491	−29.246	−21.313	−17.829	−10.453	−20.151	−13.730	−11.022

Notes The augmented autoregressions employed in the ADF analysis select the optimal lag-order with the *t-sig* criterion of Ng and Perron (1995), setting a maximum lag-order equal to 8. The information criterion BIC_3 is employed to choose the optimal rank. $P_{\hat{e}}$ is distributed as χ^2_{42}, with 1, 5 and 10 % critical values equal to 66.206, 58.124 and 54.090, respectively. $Z_{\hat{e}}$ is distributed as N(0,1) with 1, 5 and 10 % critical values of 2.326, 1.645 and 1.282

***, ** and * imply rejection of the null hypothesis at 1, 5 and 10 %, respectively

Since $k > 1$, the estimated number of $\hat{r}_1$ stochastic trends in the common factors must be determined. We employ the filtered test MQ_f, the corrected test MQ_c and the BIC_3 criterion applied to level data in order to estimate $\hat{r}_1$

Table 6.10 PANIC analysis of log annual average hours

	Trend specification: stochastic convergence		No trend specification: deterministic convergence	
	Statistic	*p*-value	Statistic	*p*-value
Panel A: idiosyncratic component				
Bai and Ng (2004) pooled statistics				
$P_{\hat{e}}$	3.559***	0.000	1.841**	0.033
$Z_{\hat{e}}$	71.835***	0.002	56.468**	0.044
Panel B: number of common factors (k) & common stochastic trends ($\hat{r}_1$)				
No. factors (BIC_3)	2		2	
MQ_c	2		2	
MQ_f	2		2	
BIC_3 (*level*)	2		2	

	Rank test	Critical values			Rank test	Critical values		
	MQ_c^τ	1 %	5 %	10 %	MQ_c^c	1 %	5 %	10 %
$\hat{r}_1 = 2$	−3.317	−38.619	−31.356	−27.435	−1.857	−31.621	−23.535	−19.923
$\hat{r}_1 = 1$	−12.984	−29.246	−21.313	−17.829	−10.108	−20.151	−13.730	−11.022
	MQ_f^τ	1 %	5 %	10 %	MQ_f^c	1 %	5 %	10 %
$\hat{r}_1 = 2$	−0.451	−38.619	−31.356	−27.435	−0.395	−31.621	−23.535	−19.923
$\hat{r}_1 = 1$	−11.321	−29.246	−21.313	−17.829	−9.869	−20.151	−13.730	−11.022

Notes The augmented autoregressions employed in the ADF analysis select the optimal lag-order with the *t-sig* criterion of Ng and Perron (1995), setting a maximum lag-order equal to 8. The information criterion BIC_3 is employed to choose the optimal rank. $P_{\hat{e}}$ is distributed as χ^2_{42}, with 1, 5 and 10 % critical values equal to 66.206, 58.124 and 54.090, respectively. $Z_{\hat{e}}$ is distributed as N(0,1) with 1, 5 and 10 % critical values of 2.326, 1.645 and 1.282

***, ** and * imply rejection of the null hypothesis at 1, 5 and 10 %, respectively

Since $k > 1$, the estimated number of $\hat{r}_1$ stochastic trends in the common factors must be determined. We employ the filtered test MQ_f, the corrected test MQ_c and the BIC_3 criterion applied to level data in order to estimate $\hat{r}_1$

common factors. The number of common factors is determined with the BIC_3 criterion of Bai and Ng (2002) applied to first-differenced data. As for the number of common stochastic trends, we report the results obtained from the use of the filtered test MQ_f and the corrected test MQ_c of Bai and Ng (2004a) as well as the BIC_3 criterion of Bai (2004) applied to level data.[1] When the number of common stochastic trends differs across methods, we base our conclusions on the results from the BIC_3 criterion of Bai (2004) applied to level data. This is due to the fact that the rank filtered and corrected statistics normally lack statistical power to reject the null hypothesis, and as a result, they render a number of stochastic trends equal to the number of common factors. The left part of each table focuses on the results for the trend specification associated with the weaker notion of stochastic convergence, whereas the right part reports the results for the no-trend specification related to the stronger notion of deterministic convergence.

6.2.1 PANIC Analysis of Stochastic Convergence

We begin with the PANIC analysis of log real GDP per worker, whose results appear in Table 6.6. Panel A provides clear-cut evidence of stationary idiosyncratic components, since both pooled Fisher-type panel unit root statistics strongly reject the null hypothesis of joint non-stationarity in the idiosyncratic series forming the panel at the 1 % level of significance. Panel B provides clear-cut evidence of the existence of two common stochastic trends contained in the two common factors. The three procedures employed, i.e., MQ_f and MQ_c of Bai and Ng (2004a) and the BIC_3 criterion of Bai (2004), all support the same finding. Hence, the presence of a jointly stationary idiosyncratic component combined with the presence of two common stochastic trends driving the observed series of log real GDP per worker gives support to the existence of stochastic convergence among the OECD countries over the period 1970–2011. Of course, the fact that there are two common stochastic trends (rather than one) precludes the possibility of pair-wise cointegration among individual series of log real GDP per worker, which would constitute stronger evidence of stochastic convergence—since each individual series would be cointegrated with one another and hence there would be convergence among each of the pairs.

As regards the log of real physical capital per worker, Panel A of Table 6.7 provides strong evidence of stationarity in the idiosyncratic component, since the joint unit root null hypothesis is strongly rejected with the pooled inverse Chi-square statistics of Maddala and Wu (1999) and Choi (2001). In addition, Panel B provides evidence of the existence of three common stochastic trends contained in

[1] In the bottom part of Tables 6.6, 6.7, 6.8, 6.9 and 6.10, we provide the step-down testing procedures containing the statistics of the filtered statistic MQ_f and the corrected statistic MQ_c for each step, along with 1, 5 and 10 % critical values.

the three common factors identified with the BIC_3 procedure of Bai and Ng (2002). This occurs irrespective of the use of the MQ_f and MQ_c rank tests of Bai and Ng (2004a) or the BIC_3 criterion of Bai (2004) applied to level data. Thus, the presence of three common stochastic trends responsible for the non-stationarity in the observed series supports the existence of stochastic convergence driven by the $N - 3 = 18$ cointegrating vectors representing stationary linear combinations among otherwise non-stationary individual series. Hence, the evidence of stochastic convergence in real physical capital per worker is weaker than for the case of real GDP per worker that exhibited a lower number of common stochastic trends.

As far as the log of human capital is concerned, Table 6.8 reports evidence of stationarity of the idiosyncratic component (Panel A) as well as of the presence of three common stochastic trends contained in the five common factors (according to the BIC_3 criterion of Bai (2004)). Thus, the evidence supportive of stochastic convergence in human capital levels is similar to that found for real physical capital per worker, also characterised by three common stochastic trends driving the observed series.

In relation to log TFP, Table 6.9 provides evidence of a stationary idiosyncratic component (as the joint unit root null hypothesis is strongly rejected with the Fisher-type pooled statistics), in combination with the existence of a single common stochastic trend contained in the two common factors, which drives the non-stationarity of individual log TFP series. Therefore, the evidence of stochastic convergence is the strongest within the set of variables under study because there is pairwise cointegration among individual log TFP series, as given by the $N - 1 = 20$ cointegrating relationships rendering stationary linear combinations among individual log TFP pairs.

Finally, Table 6.10 presents evidence consistent with a stationary idiosyncratic component along with two common stochastic trends for log average annual hours worked, irrespective of the procedure used to determine the number of common stochastic trends present in the common factors. Thus, the evidence of stochastic convergence appears similar to the case of real GDP per worker, which also exhibited two common stochastic trends along with 19 cointegrating relationships among pairs of individual series.

6.2.2 PANIC Analysis of Deterministic Convergence

The results for the stronger concept of deterministic convergence, which requires the absence of deterministic linear trends in the specification, are presented in the right part of Tables 6.6, 6.7, 6.8, 6.9 and 6.10 for each respective series. Except for the case of log TFP, the analysis of deterministic convergence provides similar results to those obtained above for the analysis of stochastic convergence in the cases of real GDP per worker, real physical capital per worker, human capital and average annual hours worked. In these four cases, the Fisher-type inverse

Chi-square panel statistics of Maddala and Wu (1999) and Choi (2001) provided evidence of stationarity in the idiosyncratic component. This was coupled with the presence of either two common stochastic trends in real GDP per worker and average annual hours worked or three common stochastic trends in the cases of real physical capital per worker and human capital.

However, in the case of log TFP, the analysis of deterministic convergence provides completely different results from that of stochastic convergence. As Panel A of Table 6.9 shows, the pooled Fisher-type statistics fail to reject the null hypothesis of joint-nonstationarity in the idiosyncratic component. This, combined with the existence of one common stochastic trend, provides evidence of a lack of deterministic convergence and absence of pairwise cointegration among individual log TFP series for the no-trend PANIC specification.

6.3 Discussion of Results

Overall, the analysis of stochastic convergence provided strong evidence of convergence patterns in the series of log TFP, as given by the existence of pairwise cointegration among individual series, as well as weaker evidence of convergence in real GDP per worker and average annual hours worked (which exhibited two common stochastic trends) and yet weaker evidence of convergence in real physical capital per worker and human capital (which exhibited three common stochastic trends). As for the analysis of deterministic convergence, there is some evidence of convergence in real GDP per worker and average annual hours worked, and to a lower extent in real physical capital per worker and human capital, but the evidence for log TFP points to a lack of deterministic convergence.

In sum, the five series are characterised by some degree of stochastic convergence, whereas only four of them (all but log TFP) display some degree of deterministic convergence over the past four decades. Given that deterministic convergence implies stochastic convergence but not the other way around, we can conclude arguing that real GDP per worker, real physical capital per worker, human capital and average annual hours worked exhibit some degree of deterministic convergence, whereas TFP series display a high degree of stochastic convergence (as given by pairwise convergence).

Chapter 7
Concluding Remarks

Abstract This chapter provides a summary of the findings and concludes by arguing that real GDP per worker, real physical capital per worker, human capital and average annual hours worked exhibit some degree of deterministic convergence, whereas TFP series display a high degree of stochastic convergence (as given by the presence of pairwise cointegration). This means that countries' TFP series are engaged in an ongoing process of narrowing of the technological gap (known as catching-up) among economies that have not yet converged. This in turn may imply that the cross-boundary adoption and convergence of technological advances is not automatic, as the view that technology is a public good would predict. In addition, most of the individual series forming the panels of real GDP per worker, real physical capital per worker, human capital and average annual hours are characterized by the attainment of long-run convergence, in which countries achieve full convergence to their respective steady-state equilibrium value.

Keywords Time-series convergence · Summary · Conclusions

The increasing availability of cross-country datasets as well as the different predictions of neoclassical and endogenous growth theory regarding cross-country convergence dynamics have brought about an intense debate among economists, economic historians and policy makers on the existence of income convergence across countries and regions. Several indicators of cross-sectional convergence are studied in the literature. They include absolute β-convergence, which implies that countries starting from a high level of output are expected to exhibit lower output growth than countries beginning with low output levels. Conditional β-convergence entails that convergence occurs after controlling for country-specific steady state factors such as accumulation rates and population growth. In addition, σ-convergence tracks the inter-temporal change in a measure of dispersion with the aim of establishing whether there is a tendency for cross-country income differences to decline over time. However, according to Quah (1993), Bernard and Durlauf (1996) and Evans and Karras (1996), cross-section tests of β-convergence are problematic.

As a response to this, Carlino and Mills (1993) proposed the notion of stochastic convergence, which implies that shocks to per capita income levels relative to the

M. Hernández Salmerón and D. Romero-Ávila, *Convergence in Output and Its Sources Among Industrialised Countries*,
SpringerBriefs in Economics, DOI 10.1007/978-3-319-13635-6_7

average of the group are temporary, thus leading the series to revert towards their respective equilibrium level of relative income. However, as Li and Papell (1999) noted, the notion of stochastic convergence implies that the log of relative income is trend stationary, and thus constitutes a weak notion of convergence. This is due to the fact that it allows for time-varying permanent differences in per capita income levels across countries through the presence of a linear trend in the deterministic component of the trend function. Hence, Li and Papell (1999) proposed a stronger definition of convergence, called deterministic convergence, implying that the log of relative income is mean stationary. Therefore, the elimination of both deterministic and stochastic trends means that income levels in one country move in parallel over the long run relative to average levels. Thus, deterministic convergence implies stochastic convergence, but not the other way around.

This paper has studied the existence of stochastic and deterministic convergence of real output per worker and the sources of output (real physical capital per worker, human capital per worker, TFP and average annual hours worked) in 21 countries over the period 1970–2011. For that purpose, we have applied a large battery of panel unit root and stationarity tests, all robust to the presence of cross-sectional dependence. By using these panel tests we can be more confident that non-rejections of the null of a unit root are not caused by the low power of conventional unit root tests of the ADF-type. A major novelty of our study compared to previous ones is that we investigate the existence of convergence patterns in the series of physical capital per worker, human capital, TFP and annual hours worked, which constitute the main sources of output.

The formal analysis of the presence of cross-sectional dependence in our panels of real GDP per worker and its sources has thrown strong evidence of cross-correlation in the innovations forming the panels studied. Therefore, we have employed the recently developed panel unit root tests of Choi (2002), Chang (2002), Smith et al. (2004), Moon and Perron (2004), Breitung and Das (2005) and Pesaran (2007), which all explicitly allow for cross-sectional dependence. We have complemented that analysis with panel stationarity tests that take joint stationarity as the null hypothesis, since rejection of the null hypothesis of non-stationarity in panel unit root testing generally indicates that at least one individual series (but not necessarily all) is converging to the average of the group. Thus, it makes more sense to have stationarity as the null hypothesis to be tested, since failure to reject the null in this case would imply that all countries are stochastically or deterministically converging. Hence, we have conducted such a confirmatory analysis with the panel stationarity tests proposed by Hadri (2000) and Harris et al. (2005), which allow for general forms of cross-sectional dependence through bootstrap methods or a factor structure, respectively.

Overall, the analysis using these panel unit root and stationarity tests has failed to provide clear-cut evidence of convergence (either stochastic or deterministic) either in real GDP per worker or in real physical capital per worker, human capital, TFP and average annual hours worked. Except for the panel unit root tests of Moon and Perron (2004) and Choi (2002), the other panel unit root statistics of Chang (2002), Smith et al. (2004), Breitung and Das (2005) and Pesaran (2007) as well as the panel stationarity tests of Hadri (2000) and Harris et al. (2005) have not generally supported the convergence hypothesis. Rather the opposite, the evidence has lent support to a lack of deterministic convergence, particularly for TFP and to a lower extent real GDP per worker, real physical capital per worker and average annual hours worked. The evidence has appeared clearly mixed for the human capital index, as given by a more balanced account of the panel procedures that support one or the other hypothesis.

The lack of consistent evidence in favour of or against either stochastic or deterministic convergence has led us to employ the less restrictive PANIC approach developed by Bai and Ng (2004a). Unlike several second-generation panel unit root tests used above such as the non-linear IV panel unit root tests of Chang (2002), the bootstrap panel unit root tests of Smith et al. (2004), the Breitung and Das (2005) test and the bootstrap version of the panel stationarity test of Hadri (2000) that only allow for weak forms of cross-sectional dependence such as contemporaneous short-run cross-correlation, the PANIC approach, by modeling cross-sectional dependence through a factor structure, is able to allow for stronger forms of cross-dependence such as cross-sectional cointegration. The PANIC approach is also superior to other factor-based panel unit root tests like those of Pesaran (2007) and Moon and Perron (2004), which either allow for only one common factor or exhibit size distortions—as the common trends may be confused with the common factors and thus removed from the data in the defactoring process. In addition, unlike other factor-based panel unit root statistics that assume the same order of integration for both the common and idiosyncratic components, the PANIC framework is flexible enough as to allow for a different order of integration in both components.

Furthermore, the analysis with panel unit root and stationarity tests other than PANIC has the conceptual limitation that, by applying the panel unit root and stationarity statistics to the log of the relative series, one has implicitly assumed a common slope of unity in the relationship between the log of a series and the log of the average. This implies that homogeneity is imposed for all i, without being previously tested before the panel unit root and stationarity tests were applied to the relative series. As argued above, a less restrictive approach consists of testing for a single common stochastic trend among a set of I(1) series. Pairwise convergence would be confirmed through the existence of $N-1$ cointegrating vectors among the N countries investigated. Thus, we have relaxed the homogeneity assumption by applying the PANIC framework to the log of real GDP per worker and its sources (rather than to the relative series) with the aim of determining the presence of a common stochastic trend driving the observed series for each respective variable. If that was the case, there would be evidence of either stochastic or deterministic convergence, depending on whether the PANIC specification includes deterministic linear trends or not.

Put it differently, PANIC can act as a cointegration framework so that the system of the N series forming each panel can be decomposed into a nonstationary part explained by the common stochastic trends ($\hat{r}_1$) and a stationary part composed of $N - \hat{r}_1$ cointegrating vectors involving stationary linear combinations of the individual series forming the panel. In short, the evidence of a common stochastic trend driving the observed series, coupled with jointly stationary idiosyncratic series, would lend support to the presence of pairwise cointegration among the individual series involved, which would be driven by a nonstationary common factor linking all individual series (involving either real GDP per worker or each of the four output sources variables) over time. This would show up as convergence patterns exhibited by the individual series over time. If the evidence, instead, indicates the existence of two common stochastic trends, there would be $N-2$ cointegrated vectors, which would imply weaker evidence of time-series convergence relative to the case of pairwise convergence. In the extreme case in which there are no cointegrating vectors, there would be N independent common stochastic trends, and zero evidence of cross-cointegration and convergence.

Taken as a whole, PANIC has improved over the other panel procedures employed in this study, thus rendering much more clear-cut evidence regarding the extent of stochastic and/or deterministic convergence in output per worker and its sources. More specifically, the analysis of stochastic convergence has provided strong evidence of convergence patterns in the series of log TFP, as given by the existence of pairwise cointegration and convergence among individual series, as well as weaker evidence of convergence in real GDP per worker and average annual hours worked (which exhibited two common stochastic trends) and yet weaker evidence of convergence in real physical capital per worker and human capital (which exhibited three common stochastic trends). As for the analysis of deterministic convergence, there is some evidence of convergence in real GDP per worker and average annual hours worked, and to a lower extent in real physical capital per worker and human capital, but the evidence for log TFP points to a lack of deterministic convergence.

Given that deterministic convergence implies stochastic convergence but not the other way around, we can conclude by arguing that real GDP per worker, real physical capital per worker, human capital and average annual hours worked exhibit some degree of deterministic convergence, whereas TFP series display a high degree of stochastic convergence (as given by pairwise convergence). This means that countries' TFP series are engaged in an ongoing process of narrowing of the technological gap (known as catching-up) among economies that have not yet converged. This in turn may imply that the cross-boundary adoption and convergence of technological advances is not automatic as the view that technology is a public good would predict. In addition, most of the individual series forming the panels of real GDP per worker, real physical capital per worker, human capital and average annual hours are characterised by the attainment of long-run convergence, in which countries achieve full convergence to their respective steady-state equilibrium value.

The finding of long-run convergence in both output per worker and the inputs series given by physical capital per worker, human capital and average annual hours worked is broadly consistent with the predictions of neoclassical growth theory, which emphasises the accumulation of inputs as the driving force behind convergence. Notwithstanding, even though long-run technological convergence has not yet been attained, the presence of catching-up in technology (as given by the finding of stochastic convergence in TFP) has in all likelihood also contributed to the attainment of long-run convergence in labour productivity. Following the insights from Bernard and Jones (1996a), who placed heavy emphasis on the role of technology transfer in driving convergence, to the extent that technological advances are made by high-income countries and then flow to technological laggards, one should expect to find long-run technological convergence among those countries adopting existing technology from the innovators, but not necessarily among those countries forming the latter group. Our results have lent support to this line of argumentation since they have not favoured the existence of deterministic convergence in TFP among OECD countries over the past four decades.[1]

In future work, it will be interesting to conduct a sectoral-level analysis of TFP convergence to determine which sector(s) might be responsible for this lack of long-run technological convergence. Using both time-series and cross-section tests of convergence at the sectoral level, Bernard and Jones (1996b, c) provided strong evidence of convergence in output per worker and TFP in services but not in manufacturing for 14 OECD countries during 1970–1987. Therefore, by applying in future work the analysis of stochastic and deterministic convergence to industry-level data over the period 1970–2011, we will be able to determine whether the lack of technological convergence in manufacturing found by Bernard and Jones (1996a, b) during the first half of the period under scrutiny carries over to the second half. This would in turn indicate that international movements of capital, mostly articulated via the manufacturing sector, have not contributed much to convergence through the diffusion of technology.

[1] See also Miller and Upadhyay (2002) for weak evidence of convergence in TFP for the panel data regressions in the high-income group.

References

Attfield CLF (2003) Structural breaks and convergence in output growth in the EU. Department of economics discussion paper no 03/544, University of Bristol, Bristol
Backus D, Kehoe P, Kydland F (1992) International real business cycles. J Polit Econ 101:745–775
Badunenko O, Romero-Ávila D (2013) Financial development and the sources of growth and convergence. Int Econ Rev 54(2):629–663
Badunenko O, Romero-Ávila D (2014) Productivity growth across Spanish Regions and industries: a production-frontier approach. Reg Stud 48(7):1242–1262
Bai J, Ng S (2002) Determining the number of factors in approximate factor models. Econometrica 70(1):191–221
Bai J, Ng S (2004a) A PANIC Attack on unit roots and cointegration. Econometrica 72 (4):1127–1177
Bai J, Ng S (2004b) A new look at panel testing of stationarity and the PPP hypothesis. In: Andrews DWK, Stock JH, Rothenberg TJ (eds) Identification and inference in econometric models: essays In Honor of Thomas J. Rothemberg. Cambridge University Press, Cambridge
Banerjee A, Marcellino M, Osbat C (2005) Testing for PPP: should we use panel methods? Empirical Econ 30:77–91
Barro RJ (1991) Economic growth in a cross section of countries. Q J Econ 106:407–443
Barro RJ, Lee J-W (2010) A new data set of educational attainment in the world, 1950–2010. J Dev Econ 104:184–198
Barro RJ, Sala-i-Martin X (1992) Convergence. J Polit Econ 100(2):223–251
Barro RJ, Sala-i-Martin X (1995) Economic growth. McGraw-Hill, Boston
Baumol WJ (1986) Productivity growth, convergence and welfare: what the long-run data show. Am Econ Rev 76(5):1972–1085
Ben-David D (1994) Convergence clubs and diverging economies. CEPR discussion paper no 922, London
Bernard AB, Durlauf SN (1995) Convergence in international output. J Appl Econ 10:97–108
Bernard AB, Durlauf SN (1996) Interpreting tests of the convergence hypothesis. J Econometrics 71:161–173
Bernard A, Jones CI (1996a) Technology and convergence. Econ J 106:1037–1044
Bernard A, Jones CI (1996b) Comparing apples to oranges: productivity convergence and measurement across industries and countries. Am Econ Rev 86(5):1216–1238
Bernard A, Jones CI (1996c) Productivity across industries and countries: time series theory and evidence. Rev Econ Stat 78(1):135–146
Breitung J, Das S (2005) Panel unit root tests under cross-sectional dependence. Stat Neerl 59:414–433
Breitung J, Pesaran MH (2008) Unit roots and cointegration in panels. In: Matyas L, Sevestre P (eds) The econometrics of panel data: fundamentals and recent developments in theory and practice, 3rd edn. Kluwer Academic Publishers, Dordrecht, pp. 279–322. Chap. 9

M. Hernández Salmerón and D. Romero-Ávila, *Convergence in Output and Its Sources Among Industrialised Countries*, SpringerBriefs in Economics, DOI 10.1007/978-3-319-13635-6

Breusch TS, Pagan AR (1980) The Lagrange Multiplier test and its application to model specifications in econometrics. Rev Econ Stud 47(1):239–253
Carlino GA, Mills LO (1993) Are U.S. regional economies converging? A time series analysis. J Monetary Econ 32:335–346
Carrion-i-Silvestre J-L, Del Barrio-Castro T, Lopez-Bazo E (2005) Breaking the panels: an application to the GDP per capita. Econ J 8:159–175
Carrion-i-Silvestre J, Surdeanu L (2011) Panel cointegration rank testing with cross-section dependence. Studies in nonlinear dynamics and econometrics, vol 15(4), Article 4. Berkeley Electronic Press, Berkeley
Chang Y (2002) Nonlinear unit root tests in panels with cross-sectional dependency. J Econometrics 110:261–292
Cheung Y-Y, Pascual AG (2004) Testing for output convergence: a re-examination. Oxford Econ Pap 56(1):45–63
Choi I (2001) Unit root tests for panel data. J Int Money Finance 20:249–272
Choi I (2002) Combination unit root tests for cross-sectionally correlated panels. In: Econometric theory and practice: frontiers of analysis and applied research: essays in honor of Peter C. B. Phillips. Cambridge University Press, Cambridge, pp 311–334
Christiano LJ, Eichenbaum M (1990) Unit roots in real GNP: do we know and do we care? Carnegie-Rochester Conf Ser Publ Policy 32:7–62
Dawson JW, Sen A (2007) New evidence on the convergence of international income from a group of 29 countries. Empirical Econ 33(2):199–230
DeJong DN, Nankervis J, Savin NE, Whiteman CH (1992) The power problems of unit root tests in time series with autoregressive errors. J Econometrics 53:323–343
De Long JB (1988) Productivity growth, convergence and welfare: comment. Am Econ Rev 78:1138–1154
Devereux M, Gregory A, Smith G (1992) Realistic cross-country consumption correlations in a two-country, equilibrium, business-cycle model. J Int Money Finance 11:3–16
Dickey DA, Fuller WA (1979) Distribution of the estimators for autoregressive time series with a unit root. J Am Stat Assoc 74:427–431
Dowrick S, Nguyen D-T (1989) OECD comparative economic growth 1950–1985: catch-up and convergence. Am Econ Rev 79(5):1010–1030
Elliot G, Rothenberg T, Stock JH (1996) Efficient tests of an autoregressive unit root. Econometrica 64:813–839
Ericsson N, Irons J, Tryon RW (2001) Output and inflation in the long-run. J Appl Econometrics 16:241–253
Evans P, Karras G (1996) Convergence revisited. J Monetary Econ 37:249–265
Feenstra RC, Inklaar R, Timmer MP (2013a) The next generation of the Penn world table. NBER working paper no 19255, July 2013, available for download at www.ggdc.net/pwt
Feenstra RC, Inklaar R, Timmer MP (2013b). PWT8.0—a user guide. Groningen growth and development centre. University of Groningen, Groningen
Feenstra RC, Inklaar R, Timmer MP (2013c). Technical guide to PWT8.0. Groningen growth and development centre. University of Groningen, Groningen
Fleissig A, Strauss J (2001) Panel unit-root tests of OECD stochastic convergence. Rev Int Econ 9 (1):153–162
Gengenbach C, Palm FC, Urbain JP (2010) Panel unit root tests in the presence of cross-sectional dependencies: comparisons and implications for modelling. Econometric Rev 29(2):111–145
Grier K, Grier R (2007) Only income diverges: a neoclassical anomaly. J Dev Econ 84:25–45
Hadri K (2000) Testing for stationarity in heterogeneous panel data. Econometrics J 3:148–161
Harris D, Leybourne SJ, McCabe BPM (2005) Panel stationarity tests for purchasing power parity with cross-sectional dependence. J Bus Econ Stat 23:395–409
Im KS, Pesaran MH (2003) On the panel unit root tests using nonlinear instrumental variables. Cambridge University, Mimeo

Im KS, Pesaran MH, Shin Y (2003) Testing for unit roots in heterogeneous panels. J Econometrics 115(1):53–74
Inklaar R, Timmer MP (2013) Capital, labor and TFP in PWT8.0. Groningen growth and development centre. University of Groningen, Groningen
Islam N (1995) Growth empirics: a panel data approach. Q J Econ 110:1127–1170
Johansen S (1988) Statistical analysis of cointegrating vectors. J Econ Dyn Control 12:231–254
Johnson S, Larson W, Papageorgiou C, Subramanian A (2013) Is newer better? Penn world table revisions and their impact on growth estimates. J Monetary Econ 60(2):255–274
Karlsson S, Lothgren M (2000) On the power and interpretation of panel unit root tests. Econ Lett 66(3):249–255
Kuo B-S, Mikkola A (2001) How sure are we about purchasing power parity: panel evidence with the null of stationary exchange rates. J Money Credit Bank 33(3):767–789
Kwiatkowski D, Phillips PCB, Schmidt P, Shin Y (1992) Testing the null hypothesis of stationarity against the alternative of a unit root: how sure are we that economic time series have a unit root? J Econometrics 54:159–178
Levin A, Lin C-F, Chu C-S (2002) Unit root tests in panel data: asymptotic and finite-sample properties. J Econometrics 108(1):1–24
Leybourne SJ (1995) Testing for unit roots using forward and reverse Dickey-Fuller regressions. Oxford Bull Econ Stat 57:559–571
Li Q, Papell DH (1999) Convergence of international output: time series evidence for 16 OECD countries. Int Rev Econ Finance 8:267–280
Loewy MB, Papell DH (1996) Are US regional incomes converging? Some further evidence. J Monetary Econ 38:587–598
Lucas RE (1988) On the mechanics of economic development. J Monetary Econ 22:3–42
Maddala GS, Wu S (1999) A comparative study of unit root tests with panel data and a new simple test. Oxford Bull Econ Stat 61:631–652
Maddison A (2003) The world economy: historical statistics. Development Center Studies, Development Center for OECD, Paris
Mankiw NG, Romer D, Weil D (1992) A contribution to the empirics of economic growth. Q J Econ 107:407–437
Miller S, Upadhyay MP (2002) Total factor productivity and the convergence hypothesis. J Macroecon 24:267–286
Moon HR, Perron B (2004) Testing for a unit root in panels with dynamic factors. J Econometrics 122:81–126
Moon HR, Perron B (2007) An empirical analysis of non-stationarity in a panel of interest rates with factors. J Appl Econometrics 22(2):383–400
Newey W, West K (1994) Automatic lag selection and covariance matrix estimation. Rev Econ Stud 61:631–653
Ng S, Perron P (1995) Unit root tests in ARMA models with data-dependent methods for the selection of the truncation lag. J Am Stat Assoc 90:268–281
O'Connell P (1998) The overvaluation of purchasing power parity. J Int Econ 44(1):1–19
Oxley L, Greasley D (1995) A time-series perspective on convergence: Australia, the UK and USA since 1870. Econ Rec 71:259–270
Psacharopoulos G (1994) Returns to investment in education: A global update. World Dev 22:1325–1343
Pantula SG, González-Farias G, Fuller WA (1994) A comparison of unit-root test criteria. J Bus Econ Stat 12:449–459
Perron P (1989) The great crash, the oil price shock, and the unit root hypothesis. Econometrica 57:1361–1401
Pesaran MH (2004) General diagnostic tests for cross section dependence in panels. IZA discussion paper series, DP no. 1240
Pesaran MH (2007) A simple panel unit root test in the presence of cross-section dependence. J Appl Econometrics 22(2):265–312

Phillips PCB, Perron P (1988) Testing for unit roots in time series. Biometrika 75:335–346
Quah DT (1992) International patterns of growth: I. Persistence in cross-country disparities. LSE working paper, London School of Economics, London
Quah DT (1993) Galton's fallacy and tests of the convergence hypothesis. Scand J Econ 95:427–443
Romer PM (1986) Increasing returns and long-run growth. J Polit Econ 94(5):1002–1037
Romer PM (1990) Endogenous technological change. J Polit Econ 98(5):S71–S102
Romero-Ávila D (2009) The convergence hypothesis for OECD countries reconsidered: panel data evidence with multiple breaks, 1870–2003. Manchester Sch 77(4):552–574
Rudebusch GD (1993) The uncertain unit root in real GNP. Am Econ Rev 83:264–272
Shin Y, Snell A (2006) Mean group tests for stationarity in heterogeneous panels. Econometrics J 9:123–158
Solow RM (1956) A Contribution to the theory of economic growth. Q J Econ 70:65–94
Smith LV, Leybourne S, Kim T, Newbold P (2004) More powerful panel data unit root tests with an application to the mean reversion in real exchange rates. J Appl Econometrics 19:147–170
Strazicich MC, Lee J, Day E (2004) Are incomes converging among OECD countries? Time series evidence with two structural breaks. J Macroecon 26(1):131–145
Strauss J, Yigit T (2003) Shortfalls of panel unit root testing. Econ Lett 81:309–313
Summers R, Heston A (1991) The Penn world table mark 5: an expanded set of international comparisons, 1950–1988. Q J Econ 106(2):327–368
Stock JH, Watson MW (1988) Testing for common trends. J Am Stat Assoc 83:1097–1107
Taylor MP, Sarno L (1998) The behavior of real exchange rates during the Post-Bretton Woods period. J Int Econ 46(2):281–312
Tomljanovich M, Vogelsang TJ (2002) Are US regions converging? Using new econometric methods to examine old issues. Empirical Econ 27:49–62

MIX
Papier aus verantwortungsvollen Quellen
Paper from responsible sources
FSC® C105338

If you have any concerns about our products,
you can contact us on
ProductSafety@springernature.com

In case Publisher is established outside the EU,
the EU authorized representative is:
Springer Nature Customer Service Center GmbH
Europaplatz 3, 69115 Heidelberg, Germany

Printed by Libri Plureos GmbH
in Hamburg, Germany